"DON'T STOP LOVING ME"

"DON'T STOP LOVING ME"

A Reassuring Guide for Mothers
of Adolescent Daughters

ANN F. CARON, ED.D.

HarperPerennial
A Division of HarperCollins*Publishers*

A hardcover edition of this book was published in 1991 by Henry Holt and Company, Inc. It is here reprinted by arrangement with Henry Holt and Company, Inc.

First HarperPerennial edition published 1992.

LIBRARY OF CONGRESS CATALOG CARD NUMBER 91-50510

ISBN 0-06-097402-8

93 94 95 96   RRD 10 9 8 7 6 5

To my daughters,
ELIZABETH *and* CATHLEEN

Contents

Acknowledgments

When Professor Joel Davitz of Columbia University's Teachers College asked me why I thought the mother-and-adolescent-daughter relationship was so unique, he sparked my search for answers and focused my research. Thank you, Joel, for your query and your guidance.

The answers might have remained unpublished without the urging of the mothers who participate in my workshops for mothers of adolescent daughters. These mothers are a constant source of stories and suggestions, and their requests for more information motivated me to write this book.

I owe the deepest gratitude to the adolescent girls I interviewed. They talked freely about their lives, their mothers, their concerns, and their pleasures. I was impressed with their wisdom and thank them for sharing their deep feelings with me.

The administrators and teachers who arranged the interviews went out of their way to provide an atmosphere that encouraged honesty, and I thank them for allowing me to talk with their students.

During the mid-1980s, interest in adoelscent girls' development was stimulated by the research of Jeanne Brooks-Gunn of the Educational Testing Service, Carol Gilligan from Har-

vard University, the late John P. Hill of Virginia Common-
wealth University, and others who are cited throughout the
book. I thank these three especially for their brilliant and
original contributions to the understanding of adolescent girls.

Molly Friedrich is a literary agent whose optimism reas-
sured me during every step of the writing process. She has
guided me through the publishing maze with unfailing warmth,
humor, and true knowledge of her profession.

I am indebted also to Cynthia Vartan of Henry Holt and
Company, who realized the importance of reaching out to
mothers of adolescent girls and with her keen editing skills
helped me to appreciate the value of each word.

When I realized that what I say in a book will last longer
than what I say in a workshop, I called upon a friend, Meredith
L. Welch, a free-lance editor and a mother of teenagers, to
be my critic. Her enthusiasm was contagious, and her per-
ceptive comments forced me to rework some concepts and to
appreciate the underlying multigenerational theme of this
book. I have benefited immensely from her good judgment
and comradeship.

My mother, Mildred Collins Fitzgerald, long ago understood the meaning of child development and practiced it by
providing her family with a safe, affectionate environment
that encouraged probing and questioning. I am forever grateful
to her and my father, John Cushing Fitzgerald.

My husband, John, has been my strongest supporter, understanding fully my need to do research and to meet dead-
lines. He is intrigued himself with mother-and-daughter
research, demonstrating to me the universality of the subject.
His love underpins and strengthens our family. Thank you,
John.

People have asked if our sons, John, Peter, Paul, and Mark,
resent my concentration on daughters. To the contrary, they
have asked good questions, offered suggestions, and have followed my progress closely. And since our sons are older than

our daughters, their adolescence provided me with a good in-house basis for comparing boys and girls. They, therefore, have helped in the writing of this book. I thank them for their constant support and affection.

Without my daughters, Elizabeth and Cathleen, I never would have thought of the relationship between mothers and daughters. Their challenges to me as adolescents and their own periods of self-doubt as young women intensified my desire to understand our mutual development and our complex bond. Elizabeth's rethinking of her childhood and adolescent experiences forced me to come to terms with my influence, both negative and positive, on her. Cathleen, a college student, read the manuscript with the eye of a young woman recently removed from adolescence. Her reactions were sometimes sharply critical and sometimes strongly reinforcing, but they were always helpful. I am enormously indebted to them both. Through Elizabeth and Cathleen I am learning what it means to be a woman. It is to them that this book is gratefully and lovingly dedicated.

Introduction

WHY MOTHERS AND ADOLESCENT DAUGHTERS?

❥ "Where were you when I needed you?" is the plea I hear most often from mothers of grown daughters when they discover I give workshops for mothers of adolescent daughters. Even women who do not have daughters join in the conversation because they remember what it was like to *be* an adolescent, and they have strong views about what their mothers should or should not have done.

And then someone will ask, "But why don't you talk about mothers and sons?" This question usually comes from a man who knows that I have four sons as well as two daughters and doesn't understand why I am more drawn to the study of adolescent girls than to that of boys. When I ask him, however, about his wife's relationship with *her* mother, or his daughter's relationship with his wife, he quickly understands. It *is* complex, he admits, and something he can't quite fathom.

A preoccupation with the mother-and-daughter relationship can capture a woman's attention at many times during her life. But the attachment takes center stage in the crucial adolescent years when the foundation for a healthy adult bond is established. And that is why I find this stage of the mother-and-daughter relationship so compelling.

I experienced my own daughters' change in attitude toward

me as they entered early adolescence. Adolescent years had been fun with our older sons. Even while the boys were involved in the usual boisterous teen activities and some daring adventures, they had remained open with us. They didn't tell me everything, but I didn't expect them to confide in me. They knew where they stood with me, and I was always direct and upbeat about them. I was pleased with myself. Parenting adolescents wasn't difficult.

Then our daughters became teenagers and my confidence plummeted. My offhand comments were taken personally. Any suggestions about clothes, room, or friends could lead to hurt feelings or confrontations. I was puzzled. I had not counted on their reaction to me being different than that of their brothers. When I gave my previously warm and loving daughters a hug, they flinched. Their brothers always accepted my spontaneous embraces.

Even more dismaying, my reactions to them also changed. I had been determined to parent girls and boys in the same way, but I found out it didn't work that way. For example, if either girl came home from a high school party smelling of beer, not only were they grounded as their brothers had been, but I was shocked and told them all my rational and irrational fears. If their brothers smelled of beer, I disapproved and they paid the consequences, but I was not surprised at their adolescent experimentation.

I searched the bookstores and libraries for "experts" to resolve my uncertainty about raising teenage daughters, but I could not find an authority on parenting who had written for mothers of adolescent girls. I attended workshops for mothers and daughters and found women exploring relationships with their own mothers, rather than with their daughters. My relationship with my mother was a good one, and I was looking toward the next generation. No one could meet my needs.

Fortunately, my daughters were looking at me critically at the same time I was looking at myself critically. I responded to my midlife reevaluation by returning to graduate school to study psychology. Motivated by my daughters' new outlooks and opinions, I chose female adolescent development as my area of concentration. The years of research were rewarding, not only in the discovery of new research about adolescent girls, but in deepening my own appreciation of this profound relationship of mother and daughter. The new studies confirm what mothers know by instinct, that girls and boys do not necessarily follow the same developmental paths through adolescence. The study of adolescent girls is an exciting new field, and I will refer to the research throughout this book.

Remembering my own need for guidance, I began to give workshops to mothers of adolescent daughters during the last years of my graduate work—the kind of workshop I was searching for when my older daughter was twelve.

The women with whom I work have confirmed my belief in the importance of adolescence. During their own adolescence, many of the women became estranged from their mothers.

"I had a very poor relationship with my mother in adolescence and it grieves me to this day," said one woman. "She never talked to me or asked me how I was doing. I am praying that I do a better job with my daughter."

More typically, women were left with ambivalent feelings about their mothers. "During my adolescence," said one mother, "there was a combination of respect and fear. I didn't quite measure up and there was pressure to emulate her."

One woman summed up the feelings of many as she said simply, "I loved her and hated her."

Their comments are not unusual. "In my experience," a principal of a junior high school wrote to me shortly after I obtained my doctoral degree, "I have seen very few mothers and daughters who, despite their love for each other, have good relationships. I suspect this is caused by the traumatic changes that take place in adolescence, by a mother's anxieties at the very real perils facing her child, and by an inability to let go of her control."

The intriguing complexity of the bond, however, goes beyond worrying about the dangers facing a child in a fast-moving society. I think it originates in the recognition of a shared gender, an unacknowledged need of a mother to convey her feelings (positive or negative) about being a woman, and her longing to entrust her traditions and values to the next generation.

Most mothers quickly discover, however, that each generation defines its own meaning and each young woman will define her own self. So a mother's attempts to impart her values may be interpreted by her adolescent daughter as efforts to control her. Knowing how to balance her responsibility as a mother with her daughter's need for individuality is the challenge.

Adolescent girls are more concerned than boys in developing and maintaining relationships, and that includes their relationship with their mothers. This finding emerges time and time again in the new research, and the voices of the girls heard throughout this book reflect this involvement. While boys tend to discover themselves more through their activities, adolescent girls are likely to learn about themselves through their relationships with others.

The present-day mothers of adolescent girls have an added challenge. They benefited from the women's movement, which raised their expectations of what they could accomplish. Now, as their daughters edge toward adolescence, these mothers are confronted with guiding girls through a different environment than they—or their mothers—experienced. Until now, there have been no guidelines.

While the women are confident that their daughters will also benefit from new opportunities, they are stymied by the traditional fears that plague all mothers of adolescent girls. These fears include not only the old worry of unwanted pregnancy, but the new specter of drug or alcohol use, the devastation of date rape, and the disintegration caused by eating disorders. They do not want to shackle their daughters, yet they wonder about their daughters' ability to meet the demands placed upon them. They vacillate between their daughters' need for independence and need for safety. They want their daughters to develop into women who can handle everything, but they hesitate because there seem to be so many dangers out there.

Above all, they long to have a close relationship with their daughters, to share their lives while respecting their individualities. As women know from their own relationship with their mothers, this closeness can be suffocating or it can be liberating. The right balance does not happen automatically. It must be worked on.

When I decided to write this book, I was stunned by the interest expressed by women of all ages in knowing more about this stage of their own development. I was told stories by women who were able to pinpoint a certain time in their adolescence that was a turning point in their relationship with their mothers. A woman told me that on her fifteenth birthday her mother gave her a lifelong membership in the Elaine Powers weight-control program. This fifteen-year-old knew she was receiving a clear message that her mother would never be satisfied with her daughter's figure. Years later, she still remembers her humiliation at receiving that "gift."

In contrast, a woman told me about the support her mother gave her when she became pregnant at the age of seventeen, and how her mother's strength at that time now guides her in her relationship with her own daughters. Her gratitude for being understood now helps her to understand.

Although some women were lucky enough to have mothers who knew how to handle early adolescence, or "seventh-grade uglies" as one mother called it, today's adolescent girls encounter a different world. Choices and the social expectations that go along with increased opportunities are exciting and challenging. To prepare a daughter for life in the twenty-first century, we need more than our mothers as guides; we need new ways of parenting our daughters.

I interviewed many girls for this book, asking them about possible areas of conflict with their mothers and what advice they would like me to give to mothers of adolescents. I was impressed with their wisdom, and their words are found in each chapter. Even though some girls believed their mothers hated them, the underlying message to their mothers was "Don't stop loving me."

During my workshops, I listen to the voices of concerned mothers who want to guide their daughters safely through adolescence. Their voices and their hopes for their daughters are the basis for this book. Their daughters' problems are mostly those of normal adolescents struggling to find themselves. Yet many of these mothers feel unloved by their daughters because the girls are confrontational, are not living up to expectations, or resent their mothers' affection. The mothers are tired of the bickering and arguing. They want to be loved as they are, with all their motherly imperfections. They want to say to their daughters, "Don't stop loving me."

Mothers may interpret normal adolescent behavior as rejection, and their daughters may view their mothers' responses as rejection. I think if mothers try to understand their adolescent daughters' perceptions, as hard as it may be at times, and never stop caring for them *or* guiding them, they will not stop loving each other.

This book is meant to facilitate that process. The voices of daughters, mothers, and experts are woven into a pattern that will suggest ways mothers and daughters can come to a fuller enjoyment and love of each other. Each mother-and-daughter bond is forged throughout life in a unique reflection of their early life together. Adolescence offers an opportunity to shape that bond into a lifelong adult friendship.

1

"Don't embarrass me, Mother."

ADOLESCENCE BEGINS

Another two-year-old stage?
A new look at girls • Dethronement
Like mother, like daughter? • "Dumping" on mother
The nurturing mother • Showing *her* individuality
Showing *mother's* individuality • How mothers bind
"They'll get too worried." • "Be with them."
Being "homey" • An encouraging sign
Memos for moms

7

❦ When she heard her mother was attending one of my workshops for mothers of adolescent girls, a thirteen-year-old exclaimed, "Well, they sure got that one right! If daughters needed help, they would have had workshops for us."

And how did the mothers react when they heard that typical adolescent remark? They agreed—mothers of teenage girls need all the help they can get. Once the confident parents of younger girls, they are baffled by the changes they see in their daughters. I could only commiserate as one mother described her daughter.

"She is increasingly sensitive to comments made by everyone in the family. What I say to her has less impact. She often disagrees with me, sometimes with tears and anger, or she acts bored with what I say."

This woman doesn't need to be told her daughter is becoming an adolescent. She hears it in her voice and she sees it in her eyes. A daughter may still look like a little girl, but the little-girl devotion to mother has vanished.

Mothers I have interviewed lament the loss of the affectionate child who lovingly took their hands and listened to their every word. Gone is the daughter who extolled their beauty and talent. In her place is an unreasonable critic who finds fault with her mother's hair style, clothes, cooking, and taste in men—even though the man in question is the girl's own father.

Mothers can take some comfort in knowing that almost all mothers of young adolescent girls experience the same assault. It may not be blatant—a subtle look or a deep sigh may suffice—but chances are a little girl will look at her mother differently when she becomes an adolescent.

Another two-year-old stage?

Adolescence is similar in many ways to the two-year-old stage. In her twos, a girl doesn't want interference as she struggles to put on her shoes; she wants to "do it myself." At about the same time she discovers that if she says "NO!"—especially in public—she can guarantee a reaction. Remember when she daringly wandered off, but never went so far that she lost sight of her mother?

A young adolescent girl is striving once again to "do it myself," but now what she wants to do is more unnerving and out of her mother's sight. She does not require her mother's participation or help in most of her activities, and, when given a choice, she will choose to be with friends rather than her mother. That does not mean she wants her mother to disappear completely; like the two-year-old, she checks to make sure her mother is there for reassurance.

A two-year-old crawling into her mother's lap seeks direct reassurance, while the adolescent looks in her mother's eyes and listens to her tone of voice for more elusive signals of acceptance. Although mothers know their daughters look for their approval during childhood, they are surprised that this yearning for their support continues through adolescence.

A mother's reaction to her daughter's new independent attitudes will determine the quality of the bond between them. Will their mother-daughter bond revert to the two-year-old relationship, enmeshing a girl and impeding her full psychological and emotional development? Will the bond be so weak and unconnected that the mother becomes a nonentity? Or will it be strong enough to guide the daughter through adolescence and provide a springboard of confidence into adulthood?

A new look at girls

Until recently, adolescence was taken seriously only by parents and law officials, *not* by psychologists, who were more concerned about infancy and early childhood. And if teenagers were studied, the subjects were boys, not girls.

This neglect of girls in research is being corrected by such leading social scientists as Jeanne Brooks-Gunn of the Educational Testing Service and Carol Gilligan of Harvard University. They have discovered that girls' experiences in adolescence do not necessarily mirror those of boys.

Psychologists have also learned that adolescence is more than a time of "transition." It is the second most important stage of life, right behind infancy, with its own patterns of growth and change. Parents are being advised to pay attention to the adolescent stage rather than hope fervently that it passes quickly. Its "plasticity," as Dr. Richard Lerner from Penn State describes a quality of adolescence,[1] offers mothers renewed opportunity for influence.

Psychoanalyst Louise Kaplan must have been thinking about mothers and daughters when she wrote, "Adolescent changes may have a more decisive and immediate impact on the evolution of the human mind than do the events of infancy."[2] We don't remember our infancy, but we have clear memories of our mothers' reactions to us during adolescence.

Dethronement

At adolescence, a daughter dethrones her mother. No matter how hard a mother tries to be perfect, a girl's budding puberty combined with her new ability to think of alternatives will topple mother's exalted status.

It is dawning on the adolescent that her family, and especially her mother, needs improvement. Mothers now do the dumbest things, or so their daughters think. A girl mentioned to me that her mother had made a big effort to watch her play soccer one afternoon—and what happened?

"My mom was rooting for the *wrong* team. I was like, 'Mom, *what* are you doing on that side?' She told me she was cheering for my team. I said, 'Mom, look at what color shirt I'm wearing!' So embarrassing—everyone was asking me what my mom was doing over there."

A younger girl would be thrilled to have her mother come to her game and it would not have mattered where she stood or when she cheered. The adolescent, on the other hand, is acutely aware of her mother's presence. Just as she believes that everyone is noticing what she is wearing and doing, she thinks her friends are equally conscious of her mother. She wants her mother to blend in, just the way she herself wants to blend in.

Mothers can be especially humiliating in front of friends. "Sometimes when my mother is picking us up from the movies or school she asks strange questions—like comparing mothers. 'What kind of rules do you have?' 'Should I be stricter?' 'What do your parents let you do?' 'Are you a good student?' It's embarrassing."

Carpools are often the only way a mother of an early adolescent can get to know her daughter's friends. This girl's mother was seizing the opportunity to find out more about the other girls. All her daughter wanted was a chauffeur who smiled and said nothing.

This dethronement is an exasperating time for a mother. Her daughter almost seems determined to undermine her self-confidence. Yet her daughter is just awakening to the possibility of life's alternatives, which include a better mother.

Like mother, like daughter?

Mother is dethroned, not only because her daughter is acquiring a new way of thinking, but because mother is a woman and the daughter is a girl. Because mothers and daughters tend to be so intimate during childhood, this shift from a simple to a complex and volatile relationship is all the more disconcerting for mothers.

A young adolescent girl scrutinizes her mother closely and wonders, "Will I be like my mother?" Her brother, who knows he is male, has no problem distinguishing himself from his mother, but she struggles against being identified with her mother. She desperately wants to be different.

She may even look like her mother, a thought that frightens most girls. "When I was a teenager and someone told me I looked like my mother, I would go to my room and cry," said one woman. Adolescents pray they will be better looking than their mothers, fathers, brothers, sisters, and friends, so for this woman to be told she looked just like her mother was a blow.

A girl's struggle against becoming her mother can persist

into adulthood. A quick glance through fiction, biographies, or popular self-help books about women will substantiate the pervasiveness of this fear.

"Dumping" on mother

Further, a mother is no longer venerated because she can't magically repair her daughter's disappointments. Adolescent problems are more hurtful and complex than childhood problems. Anxious and overwhelmed by her own inability to solve them, a girl takes out her frustrations on her mother.

When I was talking to a parent group at a junior high, a woman who had clearly run out of her patience with her daughter said, "My daughter blames me for everything. I worry about her negativism, her inaccurate view of things, her mindset about me. She always dumps on me when she comes home from school."

When I asked girls why they "dumped" on their mothers, their responses were fairly consistent. They said their mothers didn't understand the pressures they were under, pressures primarily from friends.

"I had a lot of problems with my friends in junior high," one sophomore said. "I'd come home in a really bad mood and I'd say something to my mom and it would get her mad and she would start yelling at me and she didn't know anything about what was going on between me and my friends."

Another girl explained why she hated junior high school. "Junior high is full of cliques. Everyone is rude to everyone else. They pick on one person one day and then two people gang up on one person." No wonder she was in a bad mood when she came home.

Girls are reluctant to reveal these kinds of predicaments to their mothers, so some days they get angry with their mother for no apparent reason and other days they just want to be left alone to recover from the school day.

As one girl told me when she tried to rationalize her behavior in junior high: "Sometimes there are times you just have to be by yourself and try to figure things out and, of course, I hope mothers know their daughters aren't trying to hurt them. It's the way it is coming out. I mean, they're still upset about something at school and the mothers will be upset about the anger. I think they should try to understand that it is anger over something else."

"It's not necessarily your mother that you're mad at," explained another girl. "It's just that you've had a bad day. You've got lots of homework. You have to clean your room and you had a fight with your friend and on top of it all, your mom expects you to walk the dog." She laughed. "How mean can you get?"

She continued. "It's easy to take out all your anger and frustration on your mother rather than your friends or anyone else 'cause your mother is always going to be there. She has to be."

How wonderful that this girl has the confidence that her mother will always "be there." The conviction that mother will not stop loving her builds a foundation for self-assuredness.

The nurturing mother

A mother's expectation that her daughter, as she grows older, will automatically and willingly join her in traditional "womanly" activities can disrupt their previously harmonious relationship.

A daughter notices that her mother nurtures, takes care of the children, and comforts the family. It makes no difference if her mother is working in or out of the home; she usually provides the emotional support for family members, male and female. Although a daughter may observe this role, she may not claim it as her own.

Her mother assumes that as her daughter becomes a teenager, she will help joyfully with family and household chores. Mothers are looking forward to a sharing of mutual interests with their adolescent girls, interests that include care of the family.

However, when a girl is going through her own adolescence, she often lacks the selflessness that is required to consider others first. Wrapped up in the egocentrism that is natural to early adolescence, she cannot understand her mother's desire for a loving, helpful daughter. Her mother is disappointed in her daughter's focus on herself. A son's egocentrism is easier to take. She expects him to be bored by household chores, to move out from under her wing, and to act independently.

When my sons fought against helping with dishes or other household chores, I insisted but understood their reluctance. However, I could not believe that my daughters would not willingly come to my assistance. I assumed it was in their nature to be cooperative in the kitchen. I learned differently.

When an adolescent girl senses her mother's need for support, she gets nervous and may withdraw. She has been expected to give more warmth and affection to her mother than her brothers and she usually has. Now she wonders about it.

"My mom wants me to be like a sweetie to her," one girl said. "It's like she's craving affection. Sometimes she acts as though if I said more things, like 'Mommy,' I'd get a lot from her." This teenager doesn't understand her mother's natural desire for affection from her children, and her mother doesn't realize that her adolescent daughter can't, or won't, satisfy that need.

Showing her individuality

An adolescent girl argues and bickers over everyday issues in an attempt to compel her mother to recognize her individuality. Sons, on the other hand, are encouraged to show their individuality, so a mother is not surprised when a son disagrees with her.

One mother, for instance, told me about a daily discussion she has with her sons. Every morning she reminds them to button their shirts and straighten their ties to comply with the school dress code. Every morning, much to her frustration, they respond with big smiles, "Sure, Mom," and go their way, unbuttoned.

Can you imagine reproaching a daughter that way every morning? She would not reply with a big smile, but with clenched teeth, protesting that no one else buttons shirts or straightens ties, so neither will she.

Expecting daughters to become more cooperative and less argumentative as they reach adolescence is wishful thinking. Cooperation will come later. For now, they are trying to proclaim their new sense of self, and that proclamation bursts forth as dissension.

When girls tell me they fight with their mothers about every little thing, I was reminded of the time I overheard my daughter tell a friend how mad I was at her. I didn't remember being mad at all. I did remember disagreeing with her and she interpreted that as being "furious." Somehow, she received pleasure from telling her friends how mad I was, as if my anger confirmed her independent ideas. So too with the girls I talked to. It's not so much that they exaggerate their disagreements; it's just that they see these arguments through their own eyes.

In her research on parent-adolescent conflict, Judith Smetana from the University of Rochester reported that mothers and their early-adolescent daughters argue most about helping around the house, fighting with siblings or friends, the amount of time spent on the phone or watching TV, about their irritating personality characteristics (like being moody), and the inevitable homework.[3] Older adolescents are more likely to argue about rules, curfews, and party activities.

One girl told me exactly why she thought there was so much bickering between her and her mother. "She's always on top of me," she said, "to clean my room, do my homework, and bring home good grades." She speaks for many girls.

Mothers see it differently. Sometimes they come to my workshops worn out from trying to keep their patience—and not succeeding. Just the night before a meeting, one woman's twelve-year-old had shrieked, "What's that awful smell?" as she sauntered into the kitchen waiting to be served dinner. Her mother, having prepared a special new dish and ready to collapse from a full day of working and mothering, was not in the mood to be accused of poisoning the family, but she said nothing. However, the next morning when her daughter asked her disdainfully, "Are you going to wear *that*?," her mother decided that was it and blew up. As she told this story, the other women in the workshop broke into laughter. One after the other they related similar comments from their daughters.

How can a mother withstand this constant disapproval, maintain her own sense of self, and at the same time understand her daughter's need to prove her uniqueness?

Showing mother's individuality

It is perhaps most important that a mother expect an increase in "talking back" as a first sign of adolescence and not take her daughter's comments too personally. Then her daughter should learn a better way to express her differences with her mother. This requires strength and an extraordinary confidence, but it is worth trying.

First, a girl has to know that her mother has feelings and expects and desires respect. A mother does not do her daughter a favor by letting her walk all over her. I have seen some women intimidated by a two-year-old. When the two-year-old becomes an articulate—or inarticulate—adolescent, what kind of direction will she receive from this browbeaten mother? Will mother capitulate to all her demands and not be able to offer guidance?

A teenage girl's new feelings and ideas must be acknowledged before she can begin to understand her mother's desire for respect. A girl will legitimately disagree with her mother many, many times. When she doesn't like something, her mother should ask her why or why not, as calmly as possible and with genuine interest. A mother can listen to her daughter's criticism or ideas and then give her own reasons why she likes whatever seems to offend her daughter.

A girl can be made to defend her opinions, but not her feelings. Her feelings and emotions are personal and shouldn't have to be defended, but she should be able to articulate her opinions.

A mother should always try to model the behavior she wants from her daughter. When she doesn't like what her daughter is wearing, for example, she can show her how to disagree. First she can ask her daughter why she likes what she is wearing and then listen to the answer. It is then possible to tell her why something else may be more appropriate, while conceding that her style does not have to be her mother's style.

A high school girl, recalling a fight she had with her mother when she was dressing for a part-time job interview, said, "I had on black stockings and black suede shoes, and when she saw me, she asked me where I was going. When I told her I was going for a job interview, she said, 'You look like a hooker.' She shouldn't have put me down like that. That day I really felt like a hooker."

What should her mother have said, I asked. She replied, "I wish she had said, 'You know you're going on a job interview; maybe you shouldn't wear that.' I would have listened to her."

This is good advice. She was willing to listen to her mother, but not willing to be labeled or "put down." Even if girls think their mothers' opinions are very funny and out of touch, they don't miss the underlying meaning.

How mothers bind

Mothers want and expect their adolescent daughters' world to expand beyond the home, and yet they want them to stay connected to the family. Most mothers successfully bridge the transition, but some inadvertently keep girls connected too tightly—a destructive pattern that may produce an unfortunate backlash in future years.

In our workshops when we discuss ways mothers bind adolescent daughters, some women recognize their relationship with their own mother. Old habits hang on and get repeated. Helm Steirlin, in his book *Separating Parents and Adolescents*, called attention to some of these habits.[4]

A mother, for instance, can do everything for her daughter, squelching opportunities for her to develop independence and self-confidence. In this scenario, she calls school rather than urging her daughter to talk to the counselor herself. She quarrels with teachers who insist her daughter perform. She arranges her daughter's social life and is always available, no matter how inconvenient it is. She places blame elsewhere when the girl gets into trouble ("We've moved so much, she's having a hard time adjusting"), and does not let her daughter feel the full consequences of her actions.

Mothers sometimes feel they have to defend their girls more than their boys because they assume girls are emotionally fragile. However, when a mother removes the possibility of facing difficult situations, she reinforces the perception that her daughter is fragile—a self-fulfilling prophecy.

A mother unintentionally delivers another self-defeating binding message when she denies a girl's feelings or perceptions. When a girl comes home and tells her mother how she hates a certain teacher or friend, and her mother says, "Of course, you don't hate her," not only is she denying her daughter's feelings; she is also saying that her own perceptions are the only valid ones.

Another way mothers may unintentionally restrict their daughters is by stressing such a strong sense of family loyalty that the girls are inhibited from exploring life outside the family. The mother depends on her daughter and expects to be her best friend ("I can't believe you told Lisa before you told me"). To keep mother happy, the girl will confide in her mother and not pay enough attention to her friends. This close attachment does not help the daughter develop self-confidence.

A daughter wants her mother's affection and love, but she does not want to be overwhelmed with it. As one girl put it, "If my mother and I could really sit down and have a decent conversation, I would tell her I love her. Not only that, I would just tell her, 'You and I are two different persons. I understand that you are going to be here for me, but I need a little room.'"

"They'll get too worried."

How do daughters go about getting that "little room" for themselves during adolescence if they feel their mothers are being intrusive? When psychologist Lucy Rose Fischer, author of *Linked Lives: Adult Daughters and Their Mothers*, asked adult women to reflect back on their adolescent years, they mused about the techniques they devised to keep their mothers at a distance. Some women, convinced that what mothers didn't know wouldn't hurt them, censored what they told their mothers.[5]

I heard about similar maneuvers from the girls I interviewed. As one girl explained, "If you tell them *everything*, they'll get too involved and worried about everything you do."

Other women in the Fischer study had chosen to confront their mothers, making their differences paramount, so mothers felt uncomfortable about inquiring at all about their activities. They used the old football adage, "The best defense is a good offense."

The closed door also effectively shuts mothers out. A mother recalled that her daughter went straight to her room after school, deliberately avoiding her. This mother later discovered that her daughter was avoiding her mother's after-school barrage of questions.

You can see how easy it is for mothers to become frustrated. They are accused of doing too much or too little. So what does work in establishing a good relationship in these beginning years of adolescence? In Chapter 4, ways of building a loving and trusting relationship between a mother and her daughter will be explored. To remain connected and develop individually is their mutual goal.

"Be with them."

Here's wonderful advice to mothers from a high school senior.

"Be with them. Take an interest in what they do. Take them seriously. Don't be patronizing. Sometimes when I'm baby-sitting, I'll think, 'What does this seventh-grader know about anything?,' but at the time you think you have it all together. I think for someone to tell them they don't is a big blow. Listen to them."

Being "homey"

This same girl offered further suggestions that I passed on to the mothers in my workshops, who agreed that, while amusing, they rang true. When asked how girls wanted their mothers to act, she said: "Motherly, at least until they [the daughters] are comfortable with themselves. I'd tell them to be as matronly as they want. Homey is preferable to glamorous. Maybe it's unfair to tell a mother to put on some comfortable shoes and take off the heavy makeup while my friends are around. But at least for the three years while I'm in this uncomfortable stage, I'd want her to dress as ugly as possible."

However unfair and unrealistic it is to tell mothers to be "homey," her message is one that I heard frequently. Girls want their mothers to be distinct from them, to be like mothers. They don't want their mothers to compete for glamour or for friends. They want them to be mothers.

An encouraging sign

At some distant point a daughter may be able to look at her mother with appreciation. It may take all of her adolescent years, but she eventually will realize that mothers have rights and feelings.

"I won't realize I'm being mean to my mother until some-one tells me," an articulate high school girl confessed. "But if I'm sitting with my friend and my friend's mother and they get into a fight, I can see so much from the mother's point of view, just as well as my friend's. And sometimes I end up getting mad at my friend. I wonder how she can treat her mother that way. I guess I do the same thing, but I just don't see it when I'm doing it."

Girls do not want to lose their mothers' affection, although they seem to spurn it. As they get older and lose their ego-centricity, they will probably tolerate their mothers' ideas. The stress that a girl feels in school and with her friends is masking her affection for her family, but if a mother can be patient, her daughter's true self will emerge again.

A twenty-five-year-old woman laughed as she recalled her adolescent fights with her mother. Their arguments were so intense, she said, that her mother was sure her daughter hated her. At one point she yelled at her mother, "How could I hate you so much if I didn't love you?" This comment really stopped her mother "in her tracks," and they both burst out laughing.

MEMOS FOR MOMS

1. Understand your daughter's need to show that she is different from you and don't take her negative remarks about you personally.

2. When she argues or disagrees, don't argue back. Ask her why or why not. She may have good reasons.
3. Listen to her uncritically.
4. Express your own opinions and emotions as calmly as you can. She should know how you think and feel.
5. Teach her how to disagree effectively. Model the behavior you want when you disagree with her, or anyone else.
6. Emphasize that it's okay to have ideas, feelings, or tastes that are not yours.
7. Give her age-appropriate responsibilities. Don't take away opportunities for growth by doing everything for her.
8. Don't expect her to confide in you as before.
9. Have hope. Some day she will understand you.
10. Keep loving her—and smile and laugh with her.

2

♥

"I got my period."

THE ADOLESCENT BODY: NEW FEELINGS
ABOUT A DAUGHTER

♥

When to start talking • The first signs
The period • Reactions • The early maturer
Acceptance of herself • Being prepared
Memos for moms

❦ "When my daughter was nine years old, she told me she had a breast lump," a mother said during a workshop. "I rushed her to the doctor, who gently informed me that the lump was a sign of approaching puberty." Two years after the event, this girl's mother could laugh about how astonished she had been by her daughter's development, and how difficult it was for her to admit that her little girl was maturing.

When a ten-year-old casually asked her mother, "What are condoms?" her flustered mother promptly explained all about menstruation and sex. The daughter wept about menstruation. "It frightened her," reported her mother. "And the sexual intercourse part was abhorrent to her." A younger daughter in the same family, however, absorbed this information with great curiosity, asked many questions, and seemed totally unfazed.

A third mother, too embarrassed to talk directly to her daughter, handed her a book and told her to come back if she had any questions. But she never asked—much to her mother's relief.

Most mothers have funny stories to tell about daughters catching them off guard and challenging them to talk about puberty. In my workshops, we explore strategies that can be used when that inevitable time arrives, and we laugh about our awkwardness, ineptitude, and reluctance in discussing an event that happens to every woman.

If a mother feels ill at ease, she should try to find the strategy she is most comfortable with. Whatever the method, whether a mother talks alone or with sisters in on the discussion, or consults a doctor, or hands her daughter a book or video, or all of the above (most preferable), a girl needs accurate information early and frequently.

When to start talking

When should mothers begin talking to their daughters about menstruation? The earlier the better. When Dr. Jeanne Brooks-Gunn examined girls' attitudes about menstruation she found that those who felt negative about their periods either were not adequately prepared or had received their information from a negative source.[1]

The mother who says, "I'll wait for the right moment" may wait forever. Something will always interfere, and girls seldom initiate conversations about menstruation. Mothers must plan the "right moment."

Schools will fill the gap, because health courses are usually offered in fifth or sixth grade, but for some girls it is too late, and others don't like what they hear. One girl described her reaction when the nurse in the health course said how wonderful it was becoming a woman: "I thought, you can't be serious. It's disgusting."

A few girls told me they had learned everything by the time they were in third grade—not from their mothers, but from a variety of sources, including one boy down the street who took great pride in being the first to inform little girls about their bodies.

To make sure a daughter gets a strong positive message about her body as well as accurate information about menstruation, the time to talk to her is before she hears it from others. It may be hard to upstage the bearer of bad attitudes, so it's best to start early, when she is eight or nine, or even younger, if very early puberty is common in the family. In some families, especially those with older sisters, younger girls and their mothers seem able to talk freely and openly about having periods.

The first signs

Although a handful of girls may have extremely early or late puberty, the *first* signs usually appear between the ages of eight and thirteen, a wide range of years for normal puberty, which is why it is important to talk sooner rather than later.

The budding of the breast is the first signal that puberty has begun. Although pubic hair may appear simultaneously or sometimes a little earlier, it is less likely to be noticed because of an adolescent girl's modesty. Even breasts may be overlooked, because a girl who is maturing ahead of her friends may hide beneath oversized shirts.

A girl will be undergoing biological and hormonal changes for the next *five* years, until her body completes its transition to that of an adult woman. Although a mother may suspect, from her daughter's new attitude toward her and the family, that adolescence has arrived, she may not be fully aware of the powerful physical changes her body is undergoing.

The budding of her breasts does not mean a girl is about to have her period, much to many mothers' surprise; that comes at a later stage of development, up to three years later. It does mean that her hormones are increasing their output and the four- or five-year process of puberty is beginning.

Puberty is not instant; it is a slow reconfiguration of the body.

A year and a half or so after the budding of the breasts and the appearance of pubic hair, a girl will start growing taller *and* wider. Her body is preparing for the first period, for menstruation. Her growth spurt may not be as dramatic as a boy's, but a mother will hear loud protests about how nothing fits anymore and how everything looks babyish.

Her voracious appetite may make a mother despair, but this is very normal. A girl *needs* body fat to trigger her periods. As her hips and thighs become fuller, and she loses her slim, little girl look, she may feel self-conscious about joining in some gym class activities. She will need added reassurance that she is normal and looks fine. What a mother can do to help her overcome her anxiety about her figure and weight will be discussed in a later chapter.

Her first period may arrive from ages nine to sixteen and a half, depending on when her breast development began. In the United States the average age to begin menstruation has stabilized during the last decade at twelve and a half years.

The period

Although the details of the monthly cycle are well known, I'm going to give a brief review that can be used when talking with a daughter. The girls probably won't be interested in all the details, especially if they are very young, but eventually they should know the correct sequence of the cycle.

Basically, there are four phases of the monthly menstrual cycle. During the *first* phase, hormones from the pituitary gland at the base of the brain send signals to one of the thousands of potential egg cells in the ovaries to begin developing.

In the *second* phase, the ovaries themselves start producing the hormone estrogen, which stimulates the uterus to prepare a new lining to receive an egg.

Seven or eight days into the cycle, the mature egg is released from the ovary. This *third* phase, the releasing of the egg, is called ovulation. With the release of the egg, another hormone, progesterone, is produced to aid in the building of the lining of the uterus. The egg slowly (about five days) makes its way down the Fallopian tube toward the uterus.

In the *fourth* and final phase of the cycle, fertilization of the egg may or may not take place. If a mature egg meets a healthy sperm, the egg will become fertilized. When that occurs, menstruation does not take place and the egg/sperm combination embeds itself in the wall of the uterus. If the egg does not get fertilized, it dissolves. Estrogen and progesterone stop being produced and the uterine lining breaks away and is shed. During this shedding, called the menstrual period, most of the lining and small amounts of blood are discharged from the body through the vagina. Because the flow is more brownish than red, the color may surprise or frighten girls and is worth mentioning. The menstrual period lasts three to six days and when it is over, the cycle begins again.

Although I use the phrase "monthly cycle," a young adolescent girl seldom has regular periods. During the first year of menstruation, some girls do not even produce enough hormones to ovulate, but just enough to cause the lining of the uterus to shed. In other words, *some* girls are not fertile during the first year, which may lead a prematurely sexually active girl to believe she cannot get pregnant—a fatal error.

When a girl gets her first period, her growth spurt slows down. Although she is just about at her adult height, breast development will continue until the end of puberty.

Because the timing of puberty is unique for each girl, some mothers become concerned if their daughters are not "average." Remember, "average" is a range of five years. A girl may have friends who are fully developed when she is still looking like a little girl, or she may be the tallest and biggest of her age group. Most mothers hope their daughters will be smack in the middle, and that is what a girl wants. Since she cannot dictate her timetable, she needs reassurance that whenever she begins to mature, the time is right for her. However, if a girl is thirteen or fourteen and has not shown any of the *first* signs of puberty, a mother should consult the pediatrician.

Reactions

Having a young emerging woman in the house requires an adjustment for most mothers. It is not always easy. "I'm trying to be more patient and understanding, thinking of her more as a *female*," one mother said.

"I hope I can accept her changes as they happen," said another. "I want to guide her in the right choices."

A mother of a twelve-year-old cheerfully reported that her daughter's puberty helped their relationship. "We went shopping for a bra and had a great time. I bought her sanitary pads and had her practice with them and we laughed a lot." This easy acceptance and ability to laugh is therapeutic for a young girl. Not all girls are lucky enough to have mothers who welcome puberty and not all mothers are lucky enough to have daughters who happily accept it.

A girl who has struggled through those growing years told me, "I was in seventh grade when I started going into puberty and gaining weight. My mom would say, 'Oh, you're becoming a woman!' and I would say, 'Yuck.' It was the worst thing to say to me. I didn't want curves. I wanted bones. I think moms should tell their daughters they look nice and leave it at that. I had some big battles with my mom at that time."

Perhaps if her mother had been less exuberant, quietly accepting the changes rather than enthusing about the beauties of womanhood, her daughter would not have felt so threatened by her female body.

Other girls remember being more relaxed and talking easily with their mothers about menstruation. "I remember the first time," one girl said. "I was going into seventh grade. We were in the car and my mom said, 'You'll probably be getting your period soon.' She explained it to me. She was never embarrassed about it." Although this mother waited too long to talk with her daughter, she was forthright, unflustered, and open to questions—a good approach.

According to a study by Wellesley College Center for Research on Women, girls express both positive and negative feelings about menstruation. Most girls in the study were happy about getting their periods because it "affirmed" the fact that they were normal women, particularly if they were on-time or late maturers.[2]

The study by the Wellesley Center found, however, that tolerating menstruation was more difficult than accepting it. Early adolescents were particularly concerned about the practical matters, worrying, for instance, about knowing what to do if they got their periods when they were at a football game or on a picnic or wondering if they would be in agony each month.

The Wellesley researchers suggest being honest with the girls—always good advice. For instance, some girls do have cramps and discomfort each month, while others may not even notice when their period comes. Girls should know there are many physical reactions to having a period and they are not unusual if their reactions are not the same as their friends. Girls who have high tolerance of their periods have been the best prepared. They know about tampons and pads, have been shown how to use them, and how to plan ahead by carrying one or the other in a purse.

A mother in one of my workshops had helped allay her daughter's fears by recounting her own experiences and fears.

"I found it was a time that I could share all the things that went wrong when I was in junior high and high school, the white skirts and thinking you're going to die of embarrassment. She did a lot of listening while I did a lot of sharing." Sharing can help a girl realize that the embarrassment she feels is natural and that if she takes precautions, having a period will not interfere with her everyday life.

The early maturer

John P. Hill, one of the first researchers to investigate female adolescence, found that mother-and-daughter relationships take a "temporary" turn for the worse after the first period. Both mothers and daughters in his studies felt less acceptance from each other, less influence, less involvement with each other, and many more disagreements.

These agitations are temporary with most mother-and-daughter pairs, with the exception of early-maturing girls. Their disagreements with mothers, Hill and his colleagues found, could persist well past early adolescence.[3]

Although a girl has no control over the timing of puberty (unless she develops an eating disorder), her age at maturation can affect her mother's attitude and behavior toward her. Girls who mature early, who are out of step with their peers, generally feel less accepted by their mothers than the on-time or late maturer.

A number of factors could account for this lack of empathy for the early maturer. Her mother may place adult demands on the girl, expecting her to be more responsible. She may be only ten years old, but because she looks older, parents and teachers expect her to act more like an adult.

Or it could be that the early maturer finds puberty itself more stressful because she doesn't share the event with other girls. She feels out of place and awkward and takes her unhappiness out on her mother. Her mother, not realizing the cause of this inner turmoil, may not empathize with her daughter, creating more friction between them.

Also, an early-maturing girl often is attracted to older girls and boys. But she does not have the social maturity of the older teenagers and can be introduced to a social scene that she is not able to handle. According to some studies, early maturers tend to ignore parents' prohibitions and get into deviant behavior more frequently than their later-maturing peers. They fight with their parents to obtain inappropriate privileges and dissension reigns.

When a thirteen-year-old is asked to join in the activities of the juniors and seniors in high school, she is flattered and anxious to accommodate. However, mothers must be equally insistent that their daughters remain in their own age group. A ten- to fifteen-year-old girl is not ready for the activities of eighteen-year-olds.

Acceptance of herself

By the end of puberty, a girl should be reconciled with her looks and her feelings about her body. She probably will be disappointed that she doesn't have an ideal body, whatever that may be, but she now recognizes that few others have a perfect figure either, a comforting thought.

A mother plays a primary role in encouraging that healthy acceptance. By making only positive comments about her daughter's figure and weight and by looking at her with admiration, she contributes to the girl's good body image. Remember how we used to gaze lovingly at them when they were children? Now is the time when girls need to be lovingly looked at again, now—with their pimples, bizarre hair styles, and cumbersome bodies. A girl is conscious of her appearance, and when her mother averts her eyes or looks at her with disappointment, she feels it. She needs to be reminded time and time again that she is loved, no matter what her bodily dimensions are.

Sometimes mothers expect the girls to eat and sleep as little as they did when they were youngsters, but that's not how it works. Remember how much she slept during her infancy and toddler stage? Not since then has she experienced such rapid growth—and she needs extra food and sleep.

Girls also need to become comfortable with the idea of being a woman. Girls I talked with who had been in serious trouble—with drugs, dropping out of school, or pregnancy—seldom received an affirmation of their womanhood during puberty. Instead, their mothers were frightened at the thought of puberty because now their daughters could get pregnant. This fear surfaced as anger. Rather than communicating delight that their daughters were growing up, they hostilely warned them to stay away from boys.

The girls I talked to in a shelter for the homeless said they never discussed menstruation with their mothers before they got their periods, and they had no understanding of what was happening to their young bodies. Their stories were like those of a generation ago when a girl would think she was dying when she began menstruating.

"When I first started bleeding, I was scared," a sixteen-year-old girl told me. "I said, 'Oh, my God, I'm bleeding.' I wouldn't tell my mother. My cousin had sent me this package and it had pads, but I didn't know what to do. I put the pad on the outside of the panties and then I put on two pairs of panties. Then I told my mother and she showed me how to use a pad. Then she wrote me a note saying, 'You're a young lady now. Keep your legs closed. Kissing gets you into trouble.'"

Another girl said: "I first had my period when I was thirteen. All my mother ever told me was to stay away from boys.
That was it. No reason why. She didn't say, 'You're a young
lady now' or 'You're mature.' She said, 'Now you can't sleep
over at anyone's house.' I didn't know anything. I had read
books and everything, but that's not the same. I even introduced myself to tampons. My mother should have explained."

Both of these girls are teenage mothers.

Being prepared

It was such a contrast to talk with girls who knew that their
mothers were willing to answer any questions. They felt a
kinship with their mothers and could speak openly about their
reactions and feelings. Some mothers told about feeling comfortable when discussing menstruation with their daughters.

One mother, describing her ongoing discussions with her
daughter, said, "We had our first talk soon after her ten-year-
old physical. We were home alone. I showed her teenage
sanitary napkins and she had a lot of questions: 'What if I get
it in school? How do I use napkins? Can I use tampons?' We
discussed what was going on during puberty, what it meant.
She even put on a napkin to see how they worked. One and
one-half years have passed and no period yet, but we still
mention it and answer any questions she has."

Her daughter was well developed by the time she was ten.
While shopping with her for the largest training bra available,
the mother thought they really should go to the ladies' department, but the girl was too embarrassed to shop there.
Showing a sensitivity to her daughter, she understood, and
they went to the junior department—a small detail but ap-
preciated by the girl.

Even if the discussions are clumsy or too late, girls do value their mothers' talking to them and sharing their feelings. Many of us have initiated bumbling discussions and wondered how we ever got into such a situation.

"She started doing this sort of birds-and-bees thing," a girl said. "I sat there and listened to the whole thing and when she finished she said something about the polliwog and I said, 'Mom, where did you get this? I had sex education in fifth grade,' and she said, 'You're kidding, I feel like such a fool,' and we started laughing."

When I asked another girl what advice she would give to mothers who were uneasy about talking about puberty, she said: "Don't make the girls feel uncomfortable about growing up; act ordinary and be as gentle as possible when talking about it. When I was that age I thought I was so cool. I could look like that on the outside, but on the inside I was very self-conscious. Like asking my mom for my first bra. When we were shopping my mom would ask me if it wasn't time to get a bra and I would say, 'No, no!'"

She began to hate the word *bra*. Then when she decided she wanted one, she couldn't bring herself to ask her mother directly. She laughs when she recalls that she couldn't even say the word.

The ability to laugh and share the embarrassment of growing up is precious. A daughter needs to hear her mother's expressions of quiet joy and satisfaction at her becoming a woman. The more comfortable a girl is with her womanliness, the easier puberty will be for her. In Chapter 10, I will address the more difficult task of talking directly about a girl's sexuality, a conversation that should be part of every mother's ongoing discussions about growing up.

MEMOS FOR MOMS

1. Tell your daughter when she is young, around eight or nine, about how her body will change in the next few years, so she will not be surprised when she or her friends begin to develop breasts and pubic hair.

2. Explain menstruation in a low-key, natural, accepting manner and let her know that you want to hear her questions.

3. Emphasize that girls begin maturing at different ages so she will not think she is abnormal if she is ahead or behind her friends.

4. Share with her the practical aspects of managing her periods, the value of good hygiene, the use of pads and tampons, and the importance of anticipating when she will need them.

5. Exhibit a positive attitude while at the same time acknowledging that some girls experience discomfort and others do not.

6. Read books about puberty. If you want her to read them, read them first, so you know their messages—the same with videos.

7. Find out when her school has its sex-education program so you can talk to your daughter well before the school program and be available to answer her questions after the presentation.

8. Show your love of her in your eyes and in your voice.

3

♥

"Don't worry, it won't happen to me."

THE ADOLESCENT MIND

♥

The myth of invulnerability
Adolescent thinking • "You don't understand."
Your problem or mine? • Conflict and closeness
Separation or connection?
"They should know we're not perfect."
Making decisions • "Why don't you talk to me?"
"She said too much." • Talking straight
Receptive listening • Memos for moms

A mother is telling her daughter about an accident the night before in which two high school students, driving too fast along a narrow road, hit a tree and were killed. Her daughter listens quietly, then turns and says, "Don't worry, Mom, it won't happen to me."

All sorts of fears plague mothers when they realize their daughters are unable to understand that what happens to others can happen to them. A mother, alarmed because her daughter has accumulated three speeding tickets in her eighteen months of driving, comes to my workshop frustrated and filled with questions: "How could my daughter be so naïve? Hasn't she seen the statistics? Kids die in cars going too fast. Does she really think she can drive too fast and never get hurt?"

Another mother recalls stories about teenagers who get hooked on drugs. Her daughter has friends who have been in rehab centers. Does she think she won't be affected if she tries drugs just for fun?

One mother reads articles to her children about teens who smoke marijuana and lose their ability to set goals. Her daughter knows drugged kids who just "hang out" around the school with no motivation. Does she see what they are smoking?

A mother talks to her daughter about kids who drink too much and lose the ability to say no to anything. Her daughter knows classmates who have had abortions. Does she connect drinking and sex? Why, then, doesn't she realize the possible consequences of what she is doing?

The myth of invulnerability

The teenage belief that "it won't happen to me" is incomprehensible to mothers and even to many adults who work with young people. Although this age group may have always thought it was invulnerable, the repercussions of that type of thinking have never been as grave as they are for this generation of adolescents. Mothers are justly concerned.

Teenagers have always wanted to try out what is forbidden, but it used to be more difficult to do so. When teens drank too much, cars were not as readily available so there were fewer accidents. Parents or public transportation brought them home and so their condition was noticed. When they had friends over to the house, mother or grandmother was home so they weren't free to enjoy the bedroom or the liquor cabinet. When they thought about buying drugs, they had to travel a distance because the drug scene was limited to certain sections of town.

But now, when cars and drugs are easily attainable and homes are empty, the opportunities to experiment are limitless. And the inability of most young adolescents to see beyond the immediate excitement of the moment turns the myth of invulnerability into a reality of vulnerability. Our adolescent children can and do get hurt.

I am frequently asked if girls today are more cautious because of their exposure to so many facts about the devastating effects of drugs, the possibility of AIDS, the association of cigarettes and cancer, the accidents from drunk driving, and so forth. Or, conversely, I'm asked if teenagers are experimenting even more recklessly today because they have become fatalistic, thinking it doesn't make any difference what they do because everything is harmful.

There is evidence that some girls have adopted an "I don't care" attitude because they feel helpless or overwhelmed. However, when I ask young college-age women what they think of the myth of invulnerability, they assure me that it is a reality during junior high and senior high years. Feeling shielded from danger, they and their friends never thought of the consequences of their behavior, even though they knew the "facts." Thus the myth warps reality even among girls who could be considered role models for successful passage through adolescence.

The belief of invulnerability arises during adolescence as a shield, safeguarding a girl from unnecessary fear. Rather than protecting her, however, it can have the opposite effect of relaxing her defenses and opening her up to dangers she cannot foresee.

Adolescent thinking

The mind, as well as the body, is undergoing rapid changes throughout adolescence. Not only do mothers have to adjust to their adolescents' new bodies; they need to become aware of psychological changes as their adolescents enter the adolescent world.

The questioning and challenging of their mothers that I mentioned in the first chapter demonstrate the adolescent girls' new thinking abilities. They used to accept everything their mothers said at face value, but now the girls can pick up the underlying meaning. They begin to think in more abstract terms, but they still connect everything to real events or persons. Girls may no longer believe, for example, that their mothers are perfect, not because they can imagine "perfection," but because they have met mothers they think are better.

Psychologists used to credit adolescents with the ability to think in abstractions, to have "ideas about ideas." Jean Piaget, a Swiss psychologist, theorized that the capacity to foresee many possibilities or outcomes of a situation, even if they are not immediate or visible, begins in adolescence.[1] Researchers are now discovering, however, that many people never attain that high level of abstract thinking, even in adulthood.

Piaget tested his theories with mathematical and chemical tasks, and his tests showed that, yes, perhaps some adolescents can determine how many combinations of liquids can produce a certain color. But that skill does not enable them to enter an unsupervised party where everyone is trying out various concoctions and foresee what will happen when they mix different types of alcohol. Piaget's theories have not emerged from the laboratory to be tested in the lives of teenagers.

Talking with an adolescent girl plunges the listener into the immediacy of her life. She does not ponder, for instance, the effects of hazardous waste spills on tomorrow's genetic mutations; she rages about not being able to go into the lake or ocean today because of the slimy-looking water. She will work to clean up the beaches so she can go swimming again.

She doesn't think about what she'll do if she misses her next period and suspects she's pregnant, so she has intercourse because the moment seems right.

Saying that young adolescents seldom think of consequences unless they have an immediate impact is not denigrating adolescents. It is an acknowledgment of what is. That is why they need parents and responsible adults to help guide them. If they understood the ramifications of their actions, they wouldn't need to be reminded to be aware of driving fast, taking drugs, drinking, or getting pregnant.

"If my mom tells me not to touch the stove," a sophomore in high school told me, "I'm going to touch the stove to see if it's hot. I can't comprehend that this is going to happen to me, so I have to try it."

This girl reflects one attitude when it comes to taking advice from mothers. Other girls disregard the advice because they think their mothers are programmed to tell them they can't do anything. They fail to see that while many mothers want their daughters to test situations and learn how to handle themselves, they also want them to be safe. To be safe, girls must think of consequences.

"You learn from your mistakes," a girl told me, and she is right. We all learn from our mistakes, but some mistakes are too costly. If adolescents think before they act, their mistakes won't be serious. And this skill can be taught by a patient adult.

Adolescents learn alternatives to high-risk behaviors through contact with parents, young adults, youth leaders, or other teenagers whom they respect and want to emulate. A person who sets a good example, who teaches them better ways of expressing themselves, and who is genuinely fond of teenagers provides them with a role model. When an adolescent notices that the person she admires usually sets goals, she may be influenced to think about her own goals and to work toward them.

I interviewed many girls in homeless shelters and alternative schools who set high goals for themselves. They dream of being lawyers and social workers, but no one has ever showed them that to be a professional, you have to go to school, study rather than hang out, not have a baby, and avoid drugs. They cannot visualize the steps toward achieving their goal, because they do not have adults who demonstrate how to get there.

Other girls talk about wanting a commitment from the next boy they love. Do they know that commitment is reciprocal, not always easy, and includes acceptance of the other person's own dreams, hopes, idiosyncrasies? These girls often do not have adults in their lives who have experienced that type of commitment. To be a role model to an adolescent, a person must possess the qualities the girl admires and attempt to understand her adolescent thinking.

"You don't understand."

When a girl tells her mother, "You don't understand," perhaps she is right. An adolescent girl sees things from her own viewpoint, and sometimes a mother would be hard-pressed to figure out where she is coming from. David Elkind of Tufts University described adolescents as "egocentric."[2] They think they are on center stage and the world is watching what they do or say. An adolescent "knows" that everyone notices when her hair is cut a quarter of an inch. When I ask groups of mothers if they can think of times their daughters are self-absorbed, they laugh and say, "All the time."

Besides imagining she is onstage, a girl believes that everyone reasons the way she does. She "knows" everyone thinks she is dumb if she makes a mistake in class. She is not able to differentiate her views from others. This ability will come later, after she listens to her friends' opinions and comes to respect them. One of the great benefits of friends sitting around and talking is learning from one another. If a mother likes to sit around and talk with her daughter, each begins to appreciate the other's perspective. It is through relationships that a girl sees another's point of view and develops her own.

An adolescent's sense of timing also reflects her egocentricity. When she asks her mother to pick her up at a friend's house which is thirty minutes away, she doesn't understand why her mother doesn't drop everything and do it. Taking an hour or more from her mother's day doesn't bother her. Eventually, she will learn to plan those excursions to the satisfaction of everyone's timetable, not just her own, but that insight won't come without a little help from her mother. A mother has to listen to her daughter's needs (to be with friends), state her own needs (to know in advance when she needs a ride), and negotiate an arrangement agreeable to both.

Your problem or mine?

When trying to fathom adolescent minds, mothers often are told that their daughters want to assert their independence, to be free from family, and to be on their own. But I did not hear that message from girls. I heard the theme over and over again of wanting to be close to their mothers, of a willingness to share their adolescent adventures—if mother would only understand.

"One of my friends has the best relationship with her mother," a girl told me. "I wish mine was the same. She tells her mom everything."

Her friend in the same discussion said, "My mom doesn't look at things from my point of view. If she looked at it from my point of view it would be different. She doesn't understand. She tells me to make her understand, but she just can't."

Another girl interjected, "I hate it when they tell you to make them understand. I could tell my mom a million times and she still wouldn't understand."

"My mother grew up when it was a lot different," said a girl. "I don't want to tell her everything because she would lose a lot of respect for me. We have a nice relationship, we're not open, but I don't want to tell her things."

These girls want their mothers to understand them, but are convinced their parents can't see their point of view. When Judith Smetana looked at this phenomenon, she realized that the teenager and her parent may be looking at the same issue but interpreting it differently.

Smetana divided many of the adolescent-parent conflicts into moral, conventional, and personal categories. In the moral category (lying to parents, stealing pocket money from them, not sharing with the family, or injuring siblings), adolescents clearly agreed with their parents that these matters were subject to parental jurisdiction.

In other areas, agreement was not as universal. In the category considered conventional (customs, norms of the community, politeness, responsibility), many young adolescents thought these issues were personal and were not to be dictated by parents.

Smetana found that when there was a "mismatch" of parent and child on an issue, conflict followed. Cleaning the bedroom, for instance, was rated a personal problem by many more teenagers than parents. Parents deemed cleaning the room a traditional way of cooperating in a family. The adolescent thought it was her room, so she could do what she wanted.[3]

Applying this structure to more serious conflicts in adolescence helped me understand how mothers and their daughters may be viewing the same situation from different perspectives. For instance, some adolescents consider sexual activity their "personal" business, not subject to parental or community restrictions, whereas mothers feel that sexual activity falls under the moral domain of what is right or wrong, or under the norms of the community about what is acceptable or not acceptable behavior. It is apparent that in a case like this, reaching understanding becomes more difficult.

The oldest adolescents in Smetana's study reasoned more conventionally and were more willing to recognize norms of behavior as standards for getting along in society. The girl whose room was always in shambles acquires a roommate and realizes the necessity of respect for each other's space. The girl who is sexually active becomes conscious of her responsibility in avoiding unwanted pregnancy or in the spread of sexually transmitted diseases.

As she loses her belief that the world thinks as she does, the adolescent girl finds her place in the larger community.

Conflict and closeness

Can a mother and daughter who disagree and bicker about everyday and sometimes major issues remain close to each other? The answer, which may surprise some mothers, is yes. But not every mother and daughter resolve their conflicts in such a way that they come out loving and respecting each other.

Research by Catherine Cooper of the University of Texas confirms what successful pairs of mothers and daughters know to be true. If a mother has an underlying trust and belief in her daughter and has expressed this belief with love and affection, the disagreements they have do not lead to hostility and avoidance. These mothers and daughters want to resolve their differences and are willing to express their own points of view. Discussion is *not* cut off and is not high-pitched. They listen to each other, and a mother is not dismayed at her daughter's divergent views.

Although we used to presume all conflict indicated incompatibility, Cooper and her colleagues suggest the opposite. When adolescents realize that they can disagree, negotiate, and come to mutual understanding with their parents, they see the benefit of discussion.[4] They then may use these same skills with their friends, teachers, anyone. As they learn to acknowledge others' viewpoints, they become less egocentric.

One way a mother can help a girl become less centered on herself is to adopt a sympathetic attitude. A girl told me she wanted to tell her mother, "Sympathize with me. Stop taking the other person's side all the time."

"When I'm complaining about one thing, she's thinking about how she has the same problem, only worse," said another. "She tells me that I'm young so my problems can't be as bad as hers. It makes me not look forward to being older. She's complaining so much. I think, 'Great, it's bad for me now and it will be bad for me then.' "

If a girl does not feel a closeness with her family, then the conflicts she has with her mother can escalate to fights, with yelling and nasty words exchanged. Or the daughter or the mother can refuse to discuss anything about the subject, leaving disagreements unresolved. Neither of these ways of dealing with conflict helps a girl develop the essential skill of expressing her opinions productively. Nor do they help her lose her egocentricity.

Separation or connection?

When a girl senses that her ideas and feelings are not the same as her mother's, she is discovering her uniqueness. This process of individuation, of finding the boundaries between herself and her mother, is part of the normal growing up of adolescence.

She doesn't want her relationship with her mother to end,

but to be transformed. The desire to stay connected to her family has altered psychologists' thinking about what separation means in female adolescent development.

The task of adolescents, according to the original researchers, was to find their own "identity" by becoming self-sufficient individuals. An adolescent was meant to separate from family, these psychologists said, so she could form relationships with others—find herself first, develop relationships second.

Now we are reformulating that idea and suggesting that girls and women may form their identity *through* relationships with others. It is from interacting with others that they find their own voices. They do not find their sense of self in a vacuum without friends or family. Also, the search for identity, of knowing oneself, is not an adolescent "task" only, as was once proposed. For most women, it is a lifelong search and is not isolated from their concerns for family.

Most of the earlier research on and theories of adolescence had been drawn from work with boys and applied to girls without thought of any gender differences. Now we know that many issues, including separation from family, may be perceived differently by boys and girls. To be separate and connected are not contradictory terms in the adolescent girl's search for self-knowledge. This push-pull may continue throughout a girl's relationship with her mother—how close am I, how separate am I?

I like the way John P. Hill described an adolescent's healthy autonomy, that of "self-governance" with "attachment."[5] Rather than stressing independence, Hill grasped the need of an adolescent girl to be responsible for her own behavior (self-governance) and to remain dependent on her family.

"I can talk to my mom about more things now," said a high school junior. "She seems to think I know more. I'm willing to sit down and listen to her point of view and she's willing to sit down and listen to mine." I know this girl is achieving the balance that mothers and daughters seek, that of remaining an individual while enjoying each other's mutual support and acceptance.

"They should know we're not perfect."

Many girls believe that their mothers expect them to be perfect. When I ask mothers about this notion of perfection, they laugh because they *know* their daughters aren't perfect. However, a mother can set such high standards for her daughter that when the girl does anything wrong her mother blows it out of proportion, giving her daughter the impression that she can't do anything right.

"They should focus more on the things you do right," advised a high school girl. "There are so many things you do right and then the one little thing you do wrong, they'll attack you for it. It's not fair. Everyone makes mistakes. They should know we're not perfect."

Perhaps some of that misunderstanding comes from not talking together about what the expectations are. A mother, for instance, told me *she* had to set priorities "for her defiant daughter." I was struck by the exclusion of her daughter from the setting of priorities. If she had been setting priorities "with" her daughter, her teenager might not have been as defiant. By not having the daughter's input into her own goals, she is failing to acknowledge that her daughter is growing in capability as she undergoes the fundamental changes of adolescence.

If a mother's expectation of perfection is that her daughter automatically will do everything her mother wants, then she will be disappointed. No way is a teenage girl going to be that compliant, and often she will rebel.

"She's telling me not to like this guy," said one of these "defiant" adolescents, "and it just made me want to like him more."

Carol Gilligan of Harvard University, a well-known researcher of adolescent girls, suggests encouraging the adolescent to voice her viewpoint. In the process of exploring her thoughts, the girl realizes that she doesn't have to choose between "rebellion and submission." There is a middle ground that can be reached through discussion. "In adolescence," Gilligan says, "this discovery galvanizes energy and stimulates initiative and leadership."[6]

Initiating such discussion, however, does leave open the possibility that the girl will reject what her mother is saying and a mother will not like what she is hearing, a risk some mothers are unwilling to take. When the door to an adolescent girl's thoughts opens a crack, what she says may hurt. But in order to guide her to maturity, it is important to glimpse how she is thinking, realizing no one's thinking is perfect.

Making decisions

In her ground-breaking book, *In a Different Voice*, Gilligan challenged a theory of moral development that had been based on studies only with boys. According to this theory, morally mature persons make decisions by weighing the rights or justice of a situation, taking personal considerations out of the decision-making process.

Gilligan observed that many girls were being categorized as less mature because they were making decisions based on how the decision would affect other people, putting the decision process squarely in terms of personal relationships.

After she questioned why that personal response to decision-making was considered a less mature choice, Gilligan concluded that it wasn't. Rather, there are two equal voices of morality—a voice of care and responsibility more often voiced by girls, and a voice of justice and rights more often expressed by boys. In her book, Gilligan suggests that each mode of thinking has merit and that a morally mature person can call forth either voice.[7]

The author's insights into how many girls arrive at decisions through a more personal consideration of all the factors helped me understand the complex relationship girls maintain with their mothers, not only through the tough decisions of adolescence but throughout their lives. An adult woman wrestles with moving away because her mother will be lonely. She worries that her mother will miss being a grandmother if she decides not to have children. She wonders how to explain that she and her family will not spend their vacation with her, knowing her mother will be disappointed. These are not frivolous concerns; they are reactions to human needs.

Catherine Cooper, in her research on parent-adolescent conflict mentioned earlier, observed that family dissension *that was resolved* helped an adolescent realize the mutual interdependence of family members. Resolution showed how family members depend on one another yet remain individuals. Cooper said, "To see self-sufficiency as the hallmark of maturity conveys a view of adult life which is at odds with the human condition." Hers is a statement that most women would affirm.

"Why don't you talk to me?"

"My mom's always telling me to talk to her," confided a high school junior. "So finally one day when we were in the car I asked her why *she* wasn't talking to *me*. Then she told me she had been sitting there for ten minutes racking her brain trying to think of something to say. I thought that was something you did when you were with a guy you liked and you couldn't think of anything to say. I didn't know she had to think of something to say to me. It was so strange."

True, mothers "rack their brains" to think of a subject that their daughters won't interpret as criticism or a lecture. When I asked this girl what she said to her mother, she responded, "I was quiet for a few minutes while I was thinking about it and then I just started talking to her about little things, like what you had for lunch."

Her response touched me. Chatting away about events of the day creates a bond of comradery between a mother and daughter. Often when mothers get so much negative information about adolescents they become overanxious and forget how to relax and enjoy their daughters.

Some mothers find it hard not to see their daughters in the stereotypes portrayed in films or on television about adolescents. When a mother wants to overcome those uneasy feelings, having lighthearted and friendly conversations with her daughter helps her appreciate her child's youthfulness and strengthens their ties.

As a girl matures, a mother may find it hard to remember that her young adolescent daughter is a child and that she, the mother, is the adult. It is important for a mother to be conscious of that distinction so her daughter does not become her confidante when she is too young to assume that responsibility.

"She said too much."

A girl whose parents were divorced told me, "My mom told me before she told my dad that she was going to divorce him.

At the time I liked that, but actually I would have liked it better if they had done it together. She told me a lot and actually said too much. She changed my view of him. I'm glad mothers and daughters talk, but sometimes I think there should be a little less confiding. I was in eighth grade. I ended up talking to my grandmother a lot about what my mother was telling me and my grandmother helped me."

Judith Wallerstein, in her work with children of divorce, found girls often assume responsibility for their divorced mothers, neglecting their own normal development to stay close in case they are needed. In a single-parent home, a mother has to be especially cautious about letting her child assume the comforter role. In the natural order of family life, Wallerstein points out, the parents sacrifice for the children. In many homes, the child is sacrificing for the parents, putting her interests on hold until her mother comes through the agony of divorce. Then, when she tries to catch up to her peers, she needs professional help to unravel her feelings from her mother's.[8]

For a mother to talk freely and easily about many things in her life is a daughter's wish, but an adolescent wants her mother to keep in mind that her mother's adult problems may be too difficult for her. Adolescents want mothers to be real people and reveal some, but not all, of themselves to their children.

I asked a girl who did *not* have a relaxed relationship with her mother if she thought a mother should tell her daughter, for example, if her daughter had hurt her feelings. "I wouldn't know how to deal with it if my mother starting talking honestly with me," she said. "It's not that I don't care. It would kind of scare me away because I wouldn't know what to say. I never thought of her as human before."

Although I appreciate this girl's awareness of her own feelings about her mother, I am sad that she is not willing to see her mother as "human." A mother has to open up communications with a reluctant daughter by talking about her own feelings, about how she can feel good as well as hurt.

Talking straight

"If you tell your daughter that what she's doing is hurting you," a girl said, "it's a lot different than telling her that she has no right to yell at you like that."

Adolescent girls like direct communication and understand it. Because of their age they cannot always pick up the subtleties of a vague message and they may misinterpret their mothers' comments. They want to "read" their mothers, not try to second-guess them.

That is why sarcasm from adults really bothers them. Although they may be sarcastic with their own friends, they don't know how to decipher the caustic remarks aimed at them by adults. I heard a father express surprise that a comment he had made hurt his daughter's feelings. She was not mature enough to appreciate his biting humor.

Adolescents also value helpful rather than destructive comments. Negative and destructive comments are embarrassing, nonproductive, and, again, hard to interpret. Telling an adolescent, "You were so stupid to get into that car" doesn't help her figure out how not to be "stupid." But telling her how to avoid getting into a car when she thinks the driver is drunk ("Tell him you're going with someone else and call me") is a direct, constructive message and helps her cope with the situation the next time.

Receptive listening

There are many names given to the art of listening. I like "receptive" because it signals an openness to hearing another's message. When a girl is talking, a mother can, by the expression on her face or by nodding her head or by stating the feelings she hears from her daughter, keep the conversation going. Even saying, "Let's talk about it" or "Is there something you want to talk about?" can open up a flood.

"It drives me crazy because there's no one girls can talk to," an older adolescent girl told me. "I'm telling you to tell everyone to please listen to us. Listen. We need to communicate."

A mother who sensed her fourteen-year-old daughter's unusual concern about being late for her menstrual period asked her, "Is there something that you want to talk to me about?" Her daughter, upset and confused, poured out her feelings. She and her boyfriend were "fooling around." Could the sperm have entered her vagina? She and her mother went for a pregnancy test, which turned out negative. This mother's alertness and direct question helped her daughter through a critical time.

Remembering a girl's inability to think of the consequences makes it critical that she feel free to talk to her mother— especially when she has major relationship dilemmas during adolescence.

"I think the main thing a mom has to do is remember herself," said a junior in high school. "I remember my mom saying to me that she remembers what it was like being a teenager. We'll get into a disagreement and when it's over, she'll tell me not to worry, she got into trouble sometimes, too."

One of the first signs of the ending of adolescence is when a daughter can tell her mother, "You know, maybe you're right about that." A young woman who says that to her mother has probably heard her mother say the same words to her. Mothers and daughters do learn from each other.

MEMOS FOR MOMS

1. Be aware that an adolescent thinks that what happens to others will not happen to her.
2. Alert her to possible consequences of risk-taking behavior, keeping in mind that she may still take risks.
3. Encourage her participation in groups with leaders who are good role models and who can show her alternatives to high-risk activities.
4. Converse with her frequently and include others in your conversations. She will become less self-involved when she hears others' ideas and finds listeners for her own thoughts.
5. Promote her individuality and style while at the same time including her as an important family member.
6. Ask her why she thinks a certain way and listen to what she says. Try to understand where she is coming from.
7. Don't walk away from disagreements. Resolving arguments by listening and negotiating helps her develop the resilience needed to deal with her peers.
8. Develop a sympathetic ear for all her teenage problems.
9. Make sure your comments to her are direct and positive and that criticism is constructive, not negative.
10. Remember your feelings when you were a teenager, and enjoy lighthearted moments with her.

4

♥

"Don't you trust me?"

THE DILEMMAS OF TRUST

♥

Building trust • Start with school • Vigilant trust
Trust is not naïve. • Trust is active.
Trust can be broken. • Trusting again
Trust is not "cool parenting." • Trust is direct.
Trust is caring. • Trust is not worrying.
Trust fosters healthy guilt.
Trust builds self-confidence.
Perceived Maternal Trust Scale • Memos for moms

To say that trust is the essential characteristic in a good relationship is stating the obvious. But how can you trust an adolescent girl who is testing her parents' limits and struggling to define herself?

Trust means a reliance on the integrity or the ability of another, a dependence on someone not to let you down. It is a leap of faith, giving up control and risking the possibility that the person will not live up to your expectations. However, *if you don't take a risk, you don't trust.*

Women's magazines often feature trust questionnaires for couples ("How Much Do You Trust Him?"). Women know that every time a spouse leaves the house, there is the risk of losing him. Although most couples understand this possibility, they rely on each other's trustworthiness and don't make an issue of it.

The same applies to an adolescent. When a mother trusts her daughter, she is saying, "I believe in you. I have confidence in your ability to make good decisions. I know you are faced with a lot of opportunities not to live up to my expectations, but I know I can rely on you."

"I never had problems with my mom," said a girl. "I think it's because she trusted me so much."

"She worries about me," added her classmate, "but she basically trusts that I'll be all right."

The confidence these mothers have in their daughters did not happen automatically. Many girls told me that they had broken their mother's trust at times, and acknowledged that an honest relationship has to be worked on constantly. As one girl told me, "It is built brick by brick."

Building trust

Erik Erikson first called our attention to trust. He theorized that when a mother responds appropriately to her infant's cries, the baby learns that adults are trustworthy and can be counted on to meet her needs.[1]

Trust in adolescence is just as important as it is in early childhood. However, I believe the question in adolescence is no longer "Do I trust mother?" It becomes "Does mother trust me?"

Does my mother believe that I have the ability to become a responsible adult? Does my mother think I know enough to do my homework, to associate with the right people, to stay away from drugs? Does my mother have confidence in me?

"But wait a minute," a mother said during a workshop. "I've been stonewalled by my daughter in all sorts of confrontations because when she says, 'What's the matter, don't you trust me?' I feel forced into saying, 'Of course, I trust you,' even when I don't."

I hear similar protests from other mothers. However, a trusting relationship cannot be constructed in the middle of a heated argument. It has to be built earlier so by the time mothers and daughters are at the point of discussing parties and curfews, the expectation of responsible behavior has become commonplace.

Start with school

Where can mothers begin to trust? A great starting place is homework. Many early adolescents drop their homework responsibilities in favor of the telephone. Work that used to be finished in the early evening gets pushed back until friends are in bed and unable to come to the phone. Then the whole family hears the daughter's loud justifications for staying up until midnight or later to do homework.

Homework can provide an opportunity to demonstrate what responsibility is all about. And since it's not a personal subject, it is nonthreatening. You're not criticizing her friends, her looks, her clothes, her table manners. Also, you have a backup system among her teachers who want her homework finished.

When I asked some seventh-graders about times their mothers showed mistrust, the girls frequently mentioned nagging about homework. The girls thought those constant reminders meant that their mothers didn't believe that they knew enough to get the work done. They wished their mothers had instead offered to help or answer questions.

Trusting her to do her homework means *expecting* her to complete her assignments. If she understands that homework is a continuation of her main nine-to-three job, discussions will be easier. Explain that doing well in school is a high parental value. Discuss it often, *not* when it is midnight and she is still procrastinating, but in quieter, more relaxed moments. Use the word *job* and compare her schoolwork to your own work.

One of the hardest homework problems I tackled was learning to accept my children's style of learning. They always did their homework with a radio or tape going full blast. No way could I work like that. The noise level did not interfere with their concentration; they said it aided them, and since their grades were not affected, I had to concede.

Vigilant trust

As a daughter grows older, issues of trust center on what she is doing when she is away from home, not what she is doing in the next room. *Vigilant trust* describes the type of trust that I am convinced works with adolescents. Vigilant means "keenly watchful to detect danger or trouble," and that is what mothers have to be.

Being vigilant doesn't mean trusting less, but it does mean trusting correctly. Mothers have to believe in their daughters, unless there are clear signs of violations of trust, and mothers should recognize those signs.

For instance, do you know what marijuana smells like? Do you know the look of a hangover? Are you alert to signs of sexual activity? Do you know who is calling your daughter? Could you notice a sudden influx of new clothes, cosmetics, or jewelry?

Vigilant trusting is hands-on parenting. It does not mean intrusive parenting, but it means an awareness of a daughter's activities, moods, friends, attitudes, and her well-being. Vigilant trust is caring.

In some families, even those who can afford more than one phone line, only one line comes into the house. There may be many extensions, but one line, because the mothers want to know who is calling their children. A mother should not listen in on the conversations, but she should answer the phone once in a while and become familiar with voices. If a girl is receiving strange phone calls, her mother should be aware of them. Involvement with drugs sometimes becomes apparent through telephone usage.

Trust is not naïve.

When I was visiting a drug rehabilitation center, a young girl told me that her mother trusted too much. Her mother was gullible and believed every excuse the girl gave for her irrational and dangerous behavior. The evidence of drug abuse was there, but she chose to ignore it. This is not trust; it is neglect.

"Yeah," a girl told me. "Trust is like your mother thinks you're mature enough and you're both aware of what's going on. Naïve is like they don't even know what's going on at parties."

Trust is active.

Vigilant trust means taking time to find out the social scene in the community by going to school meetings, talking to other mothers, reading the local newspapers.

My children accused me of reading the police blotter in the paper because I was looking for their friends' names, and they were right. I know that teenagers get into trouble and I wanted to know the local situation.

Trust means taking time to talk and asking daughters what they think is the best way to handle difficult situations. One girl told me what she thought mothers should do: "I think parents who don't know what their kids are doing just don't care enough to find out. Say, the kid comes home and is drunk and the *parents pass it off* by pretending she's really tired. What good does that do? That's obviously not caring. I would sit up and try to talk to her. My mom does that sometimes. She's trying to see if I'm drunk."

This girl knows her mother is not naïve. Her mother realizes that she is an adolescent who may explore or experiment in areas that she cannot handle. Her mother is not gullible and doesn't look for excuses for her daughter's behavior when she breaks their agreed-upon rules.

Some mothers remember what they did in high school so they are especially alert to any signs of drinking, drugs, or shoplifting. "I guess one of the reasons my mother worries about me is that she doesn't want me to do some of the things she did in high school," said a high school junior. "I've never been in serious trouble and part of that is because my parents trust me and the more they say they trust me, the more I want to give them reasons to trust me."

The girls who talk about being trusted say in the next breath that when they said they were going to the movies in junior high school, they often didn't go to the movies but just hung around with their friends till their parents picked them up. One girl admitted that she read the movie reviews so she would have the answer if her mother asked her anything about the movie. This type of subterfuge illustrates the difficulty in trusting an adolescent.

Trust can be broken.

To have a strong relationship with a daughter, trust her, *but* be prepared to deal with broken trust. During her experimenting adolescent days she may act like a rock star one day and a preppie the next, and mothers can be going around in circles wondering what to expect. As she is trying out different roles and meeting new friends, she will test the limits that her mother and she have agreed on.

When she comes home too late, has a party when she's in charge of the house, shows signs of drinking, or has general disregard for a mother's expectations, she has to accept the consequences. Trust and accepting consequences for actions go together.

When I asked a group of mothers if they trusted their daughters, one mother of a sixteen-year-old said, "I trust her most of the time when it concerns responsibilities at home, locking the door, taking care of her room occasionally, going to work when she is supposed to, and going off to school. Yes, I trust her. When it comes to dates or parties, no. Probably because I was young once. I'm nervous about pregnancy, drugs, alcohol."

Certainly most women would share this anxious mother's concern because these are the important questions. Pregnancy and alcohol or drug abuse are going to happen when a girl is out of the house, not under mother's watchful eyes. That's why being aware of when trust is broken is critical, so our daughters know that their healthy and safe passage through adolescence is our primary concern.

Because adolescent girls are going to experiment, mothers should not be surprised if they break agreed-upon rules. Some mothers find that talking frankly with their daughters, discussing their concerns about the girls' health and safety, and listening to their daughters' explanations clears the air and brings understanding. Often just discussing the problem honestly can influence a girl's behavior. Good two-way communication is the best deterrent to risk-taking behavior.

Other mothers must take stronger measures. Grounding— not being able to go out with friends—is frequently employed when trust is broken. I think, however, that grounding has to be used cautiously to be effective. Girls have told me how much they resented their mothers when they had to miss a special event. If an event has been planned with good friends, then grounding a girl on that particular day may be too severe and may lead to less, not more, cooperation. The grounding can take place at another time. Grounding, when used sparingly, can be an effective reminder that mothers do not want their trust broken.

Girls can begin to understand the possible outcomes of their behavior when they work as volunteers. Volunteering as an aide in a hospital, for instance, exposes a girl to the crippling effects of drunk driving and can be a more effective deterrent than grounding. There's nothing quite like helping a young mother with babies to convince a girl that taking care of babies is a full-time job. Serving dinner in a homeless shelter can make her aware of her own blessings. Good ideas and opportunities exist in most communities for hands-on life experience.

Trusting again

One of the hardest things for parents to do is reinstate trust. I can't emphasize enough how essential it is to tell a daughter she can be trusted again. No matter how many times a mother's confidence is broken, trust again—after a girl fully understands her responsibilities.

Researchers such as Julian Rotter of the University of Connecticut have found that a person who is the recipient of trust eventually becomes dependable, even if she has repeatedly rejected or broken someone's faith in her.[2] Persistent trusting *does* pay off.

"I really broke my parents' trust last year by throwing some parties while they were away, some major-league parties, and I was caught," a girl confessed. "My mom has forgiven me, but my dad hasn't. It's not like she is lenient. For a while it was strenuous. 'Twenty Questions.' I'd never be left alone. It got to a point when it was really bad and my mom sat down and said, 'Okay, let's begin all over.' I just couldn't believe it because *that's all I was waiting for. She said, 'Let's start over. It's a clean slate.' "

While this girl was telling me her story, I could feel her intense gratitude to her mother and her frustration with her father. Her mother sensed that the point had been made and now she could be trusted again—a clean slate.

This same girl said: "If your parents choose to forgive you, that's a really important thing. My mom forgave me for so many bad things I did last year. My mom just kept her trust and forgave me, and now I forgive so many more people."

Notice this girl said, "It's not like she's lenient." Vigilant trust lets a girl know that her mother cares about what time she will be home and cares if she does drink, take drugs, or get involved in sex. Girls pick up that message and are grateful for the attention and trust.

Trust is not "cool parenting."

Girls distinguish between mothers who don't care what their daughters are doing and mothers who trust. There is a big difference.

Some girls were describing certain mothers as "cool." I quickly realized, however, that "cool" mothers were trying to be adolescents themselves. These mothers were mesmerized by the teen world and thought supplying kids with beer or allowing couples to spend the night would make their daughters popular, but they were wrong. These girls were not envied by their friends. In fact, girls resent mothers who cannot differentiate themselves from their daughters.

When I asked one girl, who had told me she had a good relationship with her mother, if her mother was "cool," she replied: "She never would allow me to have people over for beer if she were home or even knew about it. I'm not allowed to do anything like that. If my mother did let me do that, then I'd know something was wrong."

When a cool mother lets her daughter stay out until all hours and doesn't inquire into what she's doing, the girl gets the message very clearly that it doesn't make any difference what she does or where she is. Listen to the anger in a young person who assumes that it doesn't make any difference if she comes home or not: "My mother is young and she wants to be partying. She just got divorced and is dating this guy. She comes home and leaves money and then goes out. She never knows or cares if I go out because she's over at his house."

This girl doesn't think she is the envy of everyone because she doesn't have any hours or restrictions. She is angry that no one has expectations for her.

Another girl who was alienated from her mother said, "She never set rules. She wasn't like that. She never was a good mother at all. There are so many things I wish she would have done that she never did . . . she never cared."

It's tough to be trustworthy when no one is showing trust in you.

Trust is direct.

"I trust *you*; it's the others I don't trust" is a common response mothers make to a girl's challenge of "Don't you trust me?"

As sensible and logical as this may seem to a mother, the teenage girl does not buy it. She believes it is an excuse, a cover-up for not having faith in her.

She will respond, as one girl did, with "You don't have to trust *them*. I'm the one you live with. It's me you have to believe. What difference does it make if you don't trust the others? I'm the one who has to get along."

As another girl put it, "If you have trust, don't suspect your kids to do the worst things." She is right, but it is difficult not to suspect the worst when newspapers and television feature stories of drunk driving, teenage pregnancies, and increased use of drugs by adolescent girls.

Some girls understand their mother's predicament. "I could understand her not trusting me," explained a mature teen. "She doesn't know whether to be overprotective or trust me. It's a hard judgment call."

Can a daughter guarantee that she will not get caught up in the teen culture of experimentation? If she would only promise that, her mother would not have to worry about her. Few girls are willing to give their mothers that guarantee. That is where trust comes in.

Trust is caring.

A girl restated her friend's feelings when she said, "I think the most important thing between mother and daughter is trust. As long as you have your mother's trust, everything will be all right. If they don't trust you, they're going to be questioning you."

Girls think normal questions are intrusive, much to their mothers' despair. Where are you going? Who are you going with? What are you going to do when you get there? Who else will be there? What time will you be home? This type of staccato questioning drives most teenagers crazy. (Wouldn't it test our patience if we were interrogated like that by our mothers?)

If a mother asks the same questions in the course of a conversation, she seems reasonable and well within her rights. When a daughter interprets the questions as an interest in what she is doing, an atmosphere of sharing and trust prevails. When she construes them as prying to make sure she is behaving, she becomes defensive and uses the old ploy of "What's the matter, don't you trust me?"

A girl who usually felt comfortable talking to her mother got mad when her mother wanted to know what she was doing that night. Then she realized that her mother was genuinely interested in what was happening.

"At first I felt she didn't trust me," she said. "But after a while it started growing on me that she was caring about me and wondering where I was. I know that when I'm a parent I will want to know where my kid is."

Girls who hate their mothers' queries are girls whose only conversations with their mothers seem to center on what restrictions are being imposed. When a mother and daughter discuss day-to-day happenings in a friendly, sharing manner, they will get used to asking and answering each other's questions.

"Questioning a little bit is okay because sometimes kids aren't going to volunteer information," advised a high school senior. "If you want to talk to them at all you've got to question, but only up to a certain point and then sit back and wait."

Great advice from a girl who realizes that each young teenager has her own way of maintaining distance from her mother. Mothers have to pace themselves, be patient, and wait for a girl to open up.

Trust is not worrying.

Sometimes the reason for a mother's frantic interrogation is that she is worried, not only about what her daughter might do, but that something disastrous might happen to her when she is out of sight. That worry is natural. However, there are events over which we have no control. Many times we just have to bite our tongues and not project our fears onto our daughters.

I remember when my daughter commuted into the city, an hour and a half each way, to take dance classes. She was fourteen, and we had hoped that she would love our local high school and its activities and not want to leave town every afternoon. However, she decided unequivocally that she wanted to be a dancer.

Her determination won out. I traveled the route with her to make sure she knew where to get off the train, knew exactly what corners to walk to, what bus to take, and what to do in an emergency.

Many an evening I worried when she had missed a train or it was delayed. I called the dance studio to make sure she left on time and I would try to recall what she was wearing that day. My imagination ran wild when there was any disruption in the routine.

However, I tried not to let her know my irrational fears. She was doing something she loved and she was successful. If she knew that I was fretting, she might have felt guilty for causing worry. Instead, she and I developed confidence in her ability to pursue her dream and get around a large, unfamiliar metropolitan area.

All of us, I'm sure, have imagined the worst when our daughters reach beyond the family for their activities. I've heard mothers express concern when their daughters are walking in their own safe neighborhoods. Yes, in some places, especially where there is a concentration of drug dealers, there is cause for concern. However, often we are projecting our own fears onto our daughter, perpetuating them in her.

When I asked some girls if they would like their mothers to worry less, they responded immediately with a "yes—definitely." Then, when they thought about it a little longer, one girl commented, "If your mother doesn't worry about you at all, you don't have the love and attention you need." And another said, "She worries to a reasonable extent. That's fine with me when her worries are reasonable."

This girl said it perfectly: "Worry to a reasonable extent." Unreasonable worry, like a long lead chain, can bind a daughter to her mother and undermine her confidence in herself. Many women say their own mothers still worry about them. These women are in their late thirties and early forties and they don't like their mothers' lack of faith in them.

A friend of my daughter's had permission to drive a group from high school up to ski with us. She had been driving less than a year so I was surprised her mother allowed her to drive a car loaded with teenagers on a major road in winter, but I decided that was her family decision. We offered to drive everyone using two cars, but the new driver wanted to drive a group without adults present. My husband and I, with our daughter and one friend, arrived first, after driving the last half hour through a terrible snowstorm. Needless to say, I was frantic about the new driver. They arrived safely, much to my relief, laughing about their narrow escapes along the way.

On Sunday morning the girl's mother called and said she was extremely worried about her daughter driving home that afternoon in Sunday traffic and wanted her to leave right away. Her daughter, however, did not want to miss a day of fun and the roads were perfectly clear, no sign of snow. They argued heatedly while we all listened to one side. Her daughter never mentioned that she had successfully driven up in a snowstorm, because she knew her mother would panic. At last the daughter won the argument, stayed for the day, and was pointedly the last one to leave late in the evening.

If her mother didn't want her sixteen-year-old driving, it would have been a reasonable request. But once she had given her permission, she should have shown complete confidence in her daughter. Instead she wavered on her decision and worried the whole weekend. That was understandable, but once the girl had started driving, there was nothing her mother could do about it. This is an example of when a mother should keep quiet—and pray. She accomplished nothing, except that she started me worrying about her daughter's driving ability.

Why do I talk about worry when the issue is trust? I think they are interrelated. Trust shows confidence in a daughter's abilities. Worry eats away at that. If a mother worries about her daughter and is forever projecting her fears on her, her daughter can lose her self-assuredness.

Trust fosters healthy guilt.

Guilt went out of style for a while in psychological circles, but once again we are realizing its benefits. I don't mean an unhealthy guilt that shackles a daughter because she fears provoking the displeasure of her mother. I mean a healthy guilt that acknowledges that some things are right and some things are wrong.

"I think a lot of the reason I don't get into trouble is because I would feel bad," a junior in high school said. "My mom trusts me. If you can get to that point with your daughter, they'll think of you before they do anything wrong. They won't do it because they don't want to lose that trust."

That comment comes from a girl who gravitates toward fast-moving crowds. She is realistic in admitting that her motivation to stay out of serious trouble comes from not wanting to jeopardize her mother's trust and her own desire not to feel bad. A little bit of guilt has worked for this girl.

"My mom always trusts me," said another girl. "She knows I can't do something wrong because I'd feel guilty. It's nice if you know your mom trusts you. You feel so much better. If you don't have trust, nothing holds you back from doing wrong."

There are as many motivations for staying out of trouble as there are girls, but I was surprised to hear these girls talk about guilt along with trust.

Also, part of what moves us to action is a desire to please others. If a mother and daughter have an overall good relationship, they will try not to disappoint each other too often. When a mother promises to go to her daughter's soccer game, help her with a special homework assignment, or take her on a shopping trip to the mall, and forgets, she probably feels terrible.

It works the same with an adolescent girl. If she doesn't live up to an agreement with her mother, an agreement they have worked out together (an important part of the equation), she more than likely feels guilty. That guilt won't hurt her.

Trust builds self-confidence.

During one of our workshops, a mother asked, "What is the worst thing you could do to a daughter?" My immediate reply was, "Destroy her self-confidence." Two other mothers, speaking from the depths of their own experiences with their mothers, concurred. They knew the importance of helping a girl develop self-confidence.

One of the best ways to help a teenager's self-confidence is to establish a trusting relationship with her. If a mother shows belief in her daughter's abilities and inner fortitude, her daughter will feel more confident and responsible. As one girl put it, "To a certain extent mothers should show they have trust in you because that gives you self-respect. Trust means they feel you are responsible and if they think you are responsible, you will be."

The girls I interviewed were normal adolescent girls who had their share of troubled times. The girls who were happy with their relationship with their mothers seemed to share two common experiences.

First, their mothers knew the social stresses their daughters were facing; and, second, their mothers talked about these pressures with the girls and trusted them to make the right decisions.

A good combination in any young person is having self-confidence and acting responsibly. Many communication-skills courses are offered to parents. These techniques are extremely helpful, but a girl will not acquire the self-confidence needed to face the twenty-first century because her mother has learned some new method of communication. The lessons can be forgotten after a few months when it becomes too exhausting to say the right thing at the right time.

A girl's confidence in herself can come simply and easily if her mother shows basic yet vigilant trust in her during these early adolescent years.

As a girl said, "Knowing that my mother thinks I'll make the right decisions makes me more open with her so we know each other better."

PERCEIVED MATERNAL TRUST SCALE

During the workshops, I give mothers a questionnaire that I have used to assess the amount of trust an adolescent thinks she is getting from her mother. This questionnaire was developed after asking junior high girls to tell me times their mothers trusted them and times their mothers did not trust them.

From the sixty or so statements they made, some colleagues and I selected thirty that we thought best represented their feelings.

When mothers have talked with their daughters about the questionnaire, good discussions have been initiated. The statements are reproduced here for those who may want to use them as a starting point in their own discussions of trust.

Remember that these are junior high girls' perceptions, not parental perceptions. Older daughters probably have some of the same feelings about being trusted, although their concerns are more related to their social life.

MY MOTHER SHOWS TRUST WHEN

She lets me go shopping by myself.

She doesn't have someone check on me all the time.

She lets me go to parties without knowing everyone there.

She leaves me in charge of the house.

She doesn't leave a long list of rules when she's away.

She thinks I can handle most situations.

She thinks I'll tell her if my friends and I get into trouble.

It's okay if I tell her what I really think.

She lets me do things my way, even if it's not her way.

She accepts my choice of friends.

She talks about our disagreements and explains her point of view.

She doesn't keep checking on my friends.

She thinks I'll do the right things when she's not home.
If I make a mistake, she doesn't keep talking about it.
She believes me when I promise I'll do my homework.

MY MOTHER DOES NOT SHOW
TRUST IN ME WHEN

She thinks if I go to a concert, I'll do drugs.
She won't let me buy clothes I like if she doesn't like them.
She thinks I might do the bad things she hears about.
She telephones to make sure I'm where I said I would be.
She won't give me reasons when she says I can't go out.
She thinks I can be influenced by kids who get into trouble.
She keeps asking me if I did my homework.
She thinks I always drink at parties.
She sometimes checks up to see if what I said is true.
She gets frantic if I don't call her.
She blames me for things others did.
She warns me a lot about other people.
She wants me to call when I arrive where I'm going.
She keeps asking me what I did in school.
She gets nervous when she thinks of me alone on a date.

MEMOS FOR MOMS

1. Be aware of what is happening in your local adolescent social scene.
2. Discuss with your daughter your expectations for her activities and behavior.
3. Ask for her thoughts about curfews, homework, dress, alcohol, drugs, sex, friends, or whatever is your concern.

4. Agree with each other on the expectations for behavior.
5. Trust that she will live up to that agreement.
6. Be *vigilant* and know the signs of breaking trust.
7. Enforce the agreed-upon consequences of breaking trust.
8. Reestablish trust; create "a fresh slate."
9. Start from number 5 and begin again.

5

♥

"Where's Dad?"

AN INFLUENCE OR AN OBSERVER?

♥

Talking with dad • Dad as participant
Dad as an influence • Her physical changes
Using mom as a filter • Dad the protector
Divorced fathers • Stepfathers • Successful dads
Dos for dads • Memos for moms

I used to think that this generation of fathers would be able to talk more easily with their teenage daughters than my father's generation, but I was wrong. Girls today complain about the same thing I felt as a teenager. Their fathers converse once in a while about school or grades or politics, but they never bring up anything personal.

"I don't talk to him about such things because he's such a nonparent," one girl said angrily in the middle of an otherwise quiet conversation.

A friend echoed her sentiments. "They have no idea what's going on. They think we are little girls."

These teenagers are growing up in two-parent homes with fathers who are physically present but psychologically absent. Their comments substantiate the research that shows that fathers and their teen daughters seldom communicate, and daughters often feel distant from their fathers, even when they live under the same roof. It's little wonder these same fathers say they don't have problems with their daughters. They simply aren't involved in their lives.

One father told me how much he had learned from reading one of my articles. He said it helped him understand what was going on between his wife and daughter. After my first rush of pleasure at his compliment, I wondered why he hadn't mentioned *his* relationship with his daughter. I now suspect he thinks that his daughter is his wife's job.

Mothers in my workshops, sensing that their daughters want to talk with their fathers, have pleaded with me to begin father-daughter workshops. And I may, if I can round up enough fathers who do want to participate rather than observe their daughters' young lives. It would be nice to help break the tradition of mother being the active parent and father remaining the passive observer of adolescent daughters.

In a four-year study, Greer L. Fox of the University of Tennessee researched ways families divide up the responsibilities for talking to their children about sex and found that many mothers and fathers divided the job by gender. Initially, mothers talked with both boys and girls; then, with prodding, fathers took over with the sons, while mothers continued with the daughters.[1]

This division of responsibilities reinforces conventional sex roles. If dad talks about sex at all, he talks only to his son, believing that it is not "his place" to deal with his daughter's personal life. Or he believes his sole role is to back up mother, to support her by not interfering with her decisions.

A father I know has a saying framed on his desk at home: "The best thing you can do for your kids is love their mother." It's hard to argue against that; of course mothers need to be loved, but kids need more than that from their fathers. A father's love should expand when children come along; his love and attention cannot be for mother alone. This same man's daughter found an active father: when she was sixteen, she started dating a twenty-six-year-old man who monopolized her teen years and eventually married her. Now, as his daughter is struggling with a painful divorce, her father wonders what he could have done differently years ago.

In defense of dads, they can be made to feel superfluous, especially when their wives are competent mothers. Yet mothers I know, both capable and not so capable, would love to see fathers take a more active interest in their girls.

Talking with dad

Dads like to solve problems quickly rather than listen to them, and that makes it hard for them to communicate with their daughters. When a girl was describing the complications she had in meeting friends at the right time and place, her father quickly suggested a phone strategy to contact all the parties within a short time. He missed the point completely; she was having fun with the intricacies of arranging a night out. He thought he was being helpful and was surprised at her angry reaction to his suggestions.

Some dads also find it difficult to admit that their daughters can teach them something. A bright, articulate girl was upset because her father never listened to her, even when they were arguing over a fact. She called him a Mr. Know-it-all.

"If I say anything to contradict him," she said in frustration, "even if we look it up in a book and I'm totally right, he's not going to budge and change his mind. I say fine and walk away from it." I empathized with her, because in my family we keep the encyclopedia readily available in the kitchen so we can restrain our "know-it-all" males.

Other dads can be persuasive debaters, so when they tell their daughters to "give me three solid reasons why you want to drop chemistry," the girls feel tongue-tied. They learn to skirt certain issues because their own adolescent arguments sound inane compared to their dads' supposedly mature, logical presentations.

Girls also find that dads can't stand confrontations, so the girls walk away rather than getting into disputes. John P. Hill reported that although fathers interrupt their daughters more after they reach puberty, girls do not interrupt their fathers more, but "yield less, displaying a passive resistance to father's control attempts."[2] A girl may argue with her mother, but she waits out her father.

For instance, one girl told me that she, her sisters, and her mother argue riotously; it is their way of communicating, but when her father comes on the scene, "My mom and I will be yelling and my dad will come downstairs and he'll have no idea what's going on and he'll start yelling because he just wants quiet. The yelling stops and everyone goes their separate ways."

Girls know that by avoiding listening or confrontation their dads remain in the dark about their activities.

Dad as participant

I thought the expression "daddy's little girl" would grate on the sensitivities of the contemporary teenage girl, but the girls who remember having that special status were pleased. However, they discussed it in the past tense because once a girl reaches puberty, her status with dad changes. A dad who used to toss a football around with his daughter can be intimidated by the physically developing young woman who doesn't like being blocked and tackled anymore. They must find new ways of relating to each other. But what activities do girls like sharing with their fathers?

When James Youniss and Jacqueline Smollar from the Center for Study of Youth Development in Washington, D.C., asked teenage girls about what they enjoyed doing with their parents, 27 percent of the girls said they didn't enjoy doing anything with their fathers, while only 7 percent responded that way about their mothers. Puzzled by this finding, Youniss and Smollar suggest that the perception of fathers as authority figures inhibits many girls. The girls don't think they will have fun with someone who is telling them what to do or trying to control them.

In a related study, Youniss and Smollar gave teenage girls a list of twenty-two items and asked them to select the person—mother, father, female friend, or male friend—they would most likely talk with about those twenty-two subjects. The girls reported they would most likely talk with their dads about only two out of twenty-two, career goals and political beliefs.

More than 60 percent of the girls said they would be *least* likely to talk to their fathers about sex or marriage, their feelings about close male friends, or about their problems with him as father. Over 50 percent selected their father as the person they would *least* likely talk with about friends, feelings about mother, doubts about their abilities, problems at school, problems with female and male friends, or fears about life.[3]

I found similar responses. Girls I interviewed reported that their relationships with their fathers usually were one-sided and authority-based. A girl who was a good student, an athlete, and an all-round wonderful daughter lamented: "My dad thinks I always have homework. I'll come home and do four hours of homework and he'll come home and say, 'Don't you have homework?' I'll tell him I just finished. He'll say, 'Go read a book.' He wants me to be active all the time. If I'm sitting watching TV, my dad will walk up and say, 'Isn't there something you should be doing?' And then he'll offer an endless barrage of suggestions."

Many parents get nervous when teenagers sit around and seem to do nothing, but dads who try to control their daughters' activities at a time when the girls are developing their own sense of what they want to do will meet strong resistance to busy work suggestions.

A dad really interested in his teenager's development has

to get to know her. He can begin by suggesting doing something together—playing cards, washing the car, figuring out the budget, learning how to pitch a ball. She will respond to the idea of spending time with him, but not to the idea of being active just to look busy.

Dad as an influence

You may think fathers who spend so little time with their girls and have so few conversations would have little positive influence in their daughters' lives. The research is just emerging and is inconclusive, but we do know that if a mother is not meeting a girl's emotional needs, her father plays an important role.

"He understands things," confided a girl. "He accepts things better than my mom. He doesn't get mad at me like mom does. I feel more comfortable with my father 'cause he's more relaxed." If dad offers a safe haven from an overly anxious, overprotective, or disturbed mother, girls depend on him.

But a more typical problem is that most fathers are not available, physically or emotionally. Whether or not the father is living in the home, his time with his daughter is limited to snatches, grabbed on the run. This girl was close to tears as she described how she almost began confiding in her father whom she loved: "On the fifteen-minute ride home from school, he asked me if everything was going okay, because he noticed that I had been upset. I said it would take so long to tell him that we'd be up all night, but I started talking to him anyway. Then we got home and that was the end of the conversation. If it had been an hour-long drive it could have been so different."

How sad this father didn't pick up his daughter's cues. She

was ready to talk and needed his advice. And when they're ready to talk, we have to be ready to listen.

The brief moments daughters and fathers do share, those without discipline, sermons, or instructions, can be precious ones for the girls. Even if the daughter isn't talking about what is on her mind, she likes hearing about her father's work, his opinions on the political scene, or some of his youthful escapades. This sharing makes her feel special and gives her some insight into her dad. He is expanding her teenage world and she is taking it all in.

When I asked a girl to tell me about her father's influence on her, she surprised herself.

"I guess I repeat a lot of the same things my father says because I respect him so much. I took a test in which you come up with a liberal or conservative score and it was funny: I came out exactly where my father is. Even though he wasn't there influencing me, he *was* there influencing me."

Researcher John Snarey of Emory University, in a study conducted over four decades, examined the effect of a father's active participation in child-rearing on his children. His results, after studying the young adult children of 248 fathers, suggest that daughters who receive warmth and attention from their fathers during adolescence become mature and autonomous, traits particularly helpful in their occupations. And daughters who were taught physical or athletic skills by their fathers during adolescence are academically successful. Snarey describes this father-and-daughter relationship as nontraditional.[4]

A father's attention to his daughter and shooting a basket or hitting a tennis ball with her not only brings enjoyment to both father and daughter but also increases the daughter's sense of "I can do it myself."

In testimonials successful women often credit their fathers for their own determination and drive. These fathers involved their daughters in their working lives. Whether dad took his daughter to a construction site, taught her the details of the marketplace, or explained with enthusiasm why he was dedicated to his job, the girl was left with the impression that the world of work was fulfilling. When mothers and fathers encourage their daughters' involvement in their work, they are motivating their daughters to think of their own career plans.

If dads continue a childlike "father knows best" relationship with their adolescent daughters, they rapidly lose influence. A father's feelings on important questions will be rejected because he is treating his daughter like a perpetual little girl, rather than an emerging young adult. This may be considered "cute" parenting by some, but in reality it is dangerous parenting, leaving a daughter unprepared for the world of the twenty-first century.

Even if daughters complain about not being able to talk about personal issues with their fathers, there are benefits in engaging daughters in impersonal discussions. The art of rational conversation is a critical skill which a young person learns by hearing and emulating. If a daughter is able to converse with her father—and mother—about world or moral issues, she will develop her own ability to analyze and discuss. Discussing timely topics will help her formulate her own opinions. Here is a role in which many fathers feel comfortable. And it is an important one. In a flawless world, a father would initiate these discussions at the dinner table, after first listening to some personal stories of what happened during his daughter's day.

Her physical changes

Only 16 percent of the girls interviewed by Jeanne Brooks-Gunn, the leading researcher in female puberty, told their fathers when they had their first period. Interestingly, girls whose fathers were told had more positive feelings about puberty than those girls who concealed the information.[5] Ideally, a girl would tell her father herself, but since many girls find that hard to do, mother should share the news with him.

By acknowledging his daughter's new status, dad can demonstrate his interest and put her at ease. Without embarrassing her, he can simply say, "I understand you had your first period. That's great." And then he can let her continue the discussion if she wishes. His child also will be grateful if he does not tease her about her breasts, a surprisingly common occurrence. Girls are self-conscious enough without teasing.

A mother blushed as she told me how her own father had emoted about his little girl growing up. Twenty years later she still feels the embarrassment she felt then. Just as girls want their mothers to accept menstruation as a natural event, they want their fathers to take it in stride.

A chilling, tormenting experience awaits some girls at puberty. Girls who had been sexually abused spoke to me about the terrifying changes in attitude and behavior toward them as they developed a womanly figure. These girls were still enraged about their lack of protection from abuse. Their mothers believed their husbands or boyfriends' denials rather than their daughters when they were told about intrusions into the girls' bedrooms or being detained in another room. The girls begged me to tell mothers to believe their daughters.

One girl, sexually abused by her stepfather, angrily described the girls she had met in a state institution. "Most of the problems girls have is because of mothers and fathers. The mother's boyfriend or husband got them pregnant. When they told their mothers, the mothers said they were lying for attention." She asked with tears in her eyes, "How could a mother listen to a man over her daughter?"

Although abuse was not an issue for women in my workshops, a few mothers were concerned with their daughters' casualness in dress, or even lack of dress, in front of their husbands. As we talked, many women remembered their mothers telling them to keep their legs together or to go put on something decent in front of their fathers. They did not have fond memories of those conversations.

I think parents set the example for attire around the house. One girl told me that her father ran around in his boxer shorts, embarrassing her when her friends were over. She said her mother didn't run around in her bra and pants and thought her father should respect her friends. I agreed and urged her to tell her father just what she had told me.

Similarly, if a father is disturbed by his daughter's attire, *he* should tell her and not leave it up to the mother. However, if he does talk with her directly, he must emphasize only the positive. If his comments make his daughter ashamed of her body, he should stay away from the subject and let mother do the talking.

Just as they do with mothers, many girls shy away from being hugged and kissed by their fathers after puberty. Fathers who like holding their daughters on their laps can be frustrated by this rejection. However, daughters do want affection; a quick hug or a neck massage are effective ways of keeping physical contact and most girls love it.

Using mom as a filter

"My mom basically takes care of everything," stated a high school sophomore. "If my dad wants to say something to me, he'll tell mom and then mom will tell me." This girl is describing how many families operate: mom is the two-way conduit for father and daughter.

However tempting it may be to take this expedient and easy route, filtering everything through mom means that dad will never know his daughter and his daughter will never know him. A mother told me her daughter could spend ten minutes telling her a story and later tell it to her father, at mother's urging, in one sentence. I think the key here is "at mother's urging." Girls hate to be told to put on a show.

Part of the fun of listening to our daughters is hearing their adolescent exuberance. A mother is usually the first one to hear the events of the day, much more fun than hearing a watered-down version. When dad hears the story from mom, the inflection, the excitement, the passion, the anger, the joy are missing.

If a father is truly immersed in what his daughter is doing, she will tell him the same stories she has told her mother, if only to see his reaction. An adolescent loves to make an impression and dad can be a wonderful audience. Perhaps mother might have to suggest that he ask her about a particular event. A little prepping will facilitate the sharing.

I remember reading a short story about a man whose wife shielded him from his children because he had such a stressful job. They interpreted his lack of emotional involvement as indifference. And so he died a lonely widower, unable to communicate with his children without his wife there to fill in the silences.

How much better it would be for mothers and fathers and daughters to share news and stories directly. Whether it is good news about school or friends or unwelcome news that they know he won't like, daughters must get the feeling that dad is a real person.

As a woman told me, "It's unfair to keep things away from him because that's what gives a false sense of the father and the man. He takes on the negative image of someone who can't understand." This father was not told by his daughter, a sophomore in high school, about her best friend's abortion.

His wife couldn't bring herself to tell him either, so he missed the chance to help his daughter cope with her friend's unhappiness. She still thinks a lot, the girl told me, about her friend's agonizing decision, but she will never share it with her dad, even though she loves him.

This "false sense of father" struck home with me when in the middle of a discussion about boyfriends, my daughter asked me, "Do you really like dad?" The question took me back, because I thought it was obvious that I did like dad. I didn't quite grasp her meaning, first construing it as a typical adolescent comment. Then I realized that she did not really know him. He traveled frequently on business, attended community events when he was home, and had little time to get to know her. She was asking to share some of his experiences, his enthusiasm, his knowledge, and his interests so she also could grow to "like" him. We learned from her simple question that he had to begin communicating directly with her.

Dad the protector

Even if fathers do not get involved in the personal lives of their daughters, their mere presence adds stability to the girls' sense of self. A study led by Sanford Dornbusch[6] of Stanford University suggests that families headed only by mothers suffer more adolescent deviant behavior than two-parent families. The father's presence can act as a deterrent to deviance.

Several girls seemed pleased when they described their dads as "protective" (not overprotective). Even when fathers don't talk directly about protecting their daughters, girls pick up the underlying and reassuring meaning.

Sometimes the girls are amused by their dad's concern. "If

I ever had to talk to dad about sex," laughed a girl, "he'd be like, 'Where is he?' and go after him."

"Yeah," chuckled her friend. "Dads are so protective. My dad asks, 'Is he Catholic? Is he Italian? Is he rich? Is he smart?' If I say no to all those things, he'll say, 'You gotta get rid of him.' He's kidding, of course."

Divorced fathers

Single mothers who don't have the luxury of depending on dad's presence may have to rely on their male relatives or friends to fill the role of interested and caring protector. A caring man, a mentor, can help a mother guide her young daughter through adolescence. Grandfathers and uncles can be especially helpful.

A divorced father, however, can remain the protector if he is an ever-present parent to his teenage children through frequent visits and constant telephone calls to find out how they are doing. It is crucial for adolescents to know that their fathers care about them—and about their behavior. Judith Wallerstein confirms the anguish of teenagers who have lost their fathers through divorce and who think their fathers don't care about them anymore. Adolescents want their fathers to remain in close touch.[7] That unspoken yearning does not seem to be an unreasonable request. They need their fathers.

Stepfathers

A father's relationship with his own daughter may be described as "nonrelational," but with stepfathers it often becomes overly relational, and girls don't like it. The message I heard from girls to their stepfathers was "Don't get too involved with me. I'm my mother's child."

While Judith Wallerstein's research suggests that adolescence is a period of "particularly grave risk for children in divorced families," she also writes that girls experience a "sleeper" effect of divorce, feeling the consequences most acutely in their early adult years.

From my discussions with adolescent girls, however, I believe they also feel the critical effects of divorce at the moment they begin living with a stepfather. Adjusting to divorce and to a new father requires an inner strength and maturity that many girls do not yet possess.

Reactions to stepfathers are not all negative. It depends on the "situation," but most situations are, initially at least, very difficult for most girls.

Most stepdaughters still have their own fathers and they don't want someone claiming that position. "He's a nice guy," said one girl, trying to describe her stepfather. "I love him, but it feels funny 'cause I have a father. It feels real funny."

The idea that someone knows their mother so well also bothers girls. Daughters and mothers have become close during those years of a mother-only home, and frequently a girl has become her mother's confidante. As one girl testily put it, "I knew my mom long before he did. It bothers me that he thinks he knows more about my mom than I do. When it comes to my mom and her husband, I'm nothing."

A couple of girls wouldn't even say the word *stepfather*; they said "my mother's husband."

Most of the arguments between a girl and her stepfather are about control of her activities. "I want my *mother* to tell me what to do," one girl said. Girls don't want their mothers to relax after single-parenting. Yet mother may be very willing to let a man bring a "little discipline" to the home.

Her daughter, however, who probably doesn't like the idea

of remarriage, certainly doesn't see the need for more discipline from anyone and especially not from an intruder.

When I asked girls what a stepfather should do, their answers reflected their uncertainty. They said that mothers should stay in charge and stepfathers should ease their way into the family. Also, stepfathers could make the girls more comfortable by not being so amorous with their mothers—they hate that—and by suggesting ways to know and like each other better. They should take the lead in winning their step-daughters over, bearing in mind that a girl may tolerate talks with her stepfather, but not hugs.

A girl also does not want her stepfather to "butt in" between her mother and her, but if she sees that he is contributing to a more interesting or fun family environment, she eventually will begin to look at him as a person, not a stranger. Waiting for this to happen will take patience, but a happy daughter and an accepting stepfather are worth the wait.

Successful dads

In his long-term study, John Snarey not only looked at the effect of involved, nurturing fathers on children, the research I mentioned earlier, but also examined the effect of involved parenting on the father's midlife career and his ability to nurture other adults. Snarey found that "in the long run, involved fathers went just as far in their work as comparable men who were less involved with their kids." He also concluded that fathers who nurture children are more able to nurture adult relationships in midlife.[8] So fathers can have the best of all worlds: time with their daughters, success in their work, and good friends. Involved parenting does pay off—and that is good news.

DOS FOR DADS

1. Spend time with your daughter on weekends. As one girl said, "If your dad wants to spend time with you on the weekend, you know you're important."
2. Share your interests with her by talking about them.
3. Ask her what activities she would enjoy doing with you. Be ready for surprises. She may ask you to take her horseback riding.
4. Include her friends in some of your outings.
5. Include her in your "adult" conversations by *looking at her* when you talk. Ask her opinions about events in the news.
6. Ask "How are you doing?" Ask it often enough and she might tell you.
7. Remember her friends' names and ask about them.
8. Teach her your special skills, whether it's throwing a ball, washing the car, collecting baseball cards, hiking in the wilderness, painting the house, cooking, or whatever.
9. Learn a new skill with her.
10. Notice *her* special abilities and encourage them.
11. If you can't think of anything to do together at home, get involved together in community work. Clean up the neighborhood; campaign for a candidate or an issue; find out how to use a voting machine; drive the elderly; visit a nursing home. Find out the needs of your community from your local paper.
12. Listen carefully to her conversations about school, work, and friends. They are *not* trivial.
13. If she does talk about her problems, don't offer immediate solutions. Ask her what she thinks should be done. She may have the answer.
14. Remember not to tease her about her new figure. Compliments only.

15. Admit that sometimes you have doubts and fears and share how you conquered them.
16. Ask your wife how you could be of help to your daughter.
17. Love them both.

MEMOS FOR MOMS

1. Encourage your daughter to talk directly to her father so he feels included and she can see the effect of what she has to say.
2. Arrange family time so the three of you can be in the same place at the same time.
3. Plan family dinners together where everyone can share the happenings of the day and one person does not dominate.
4. Let dad know that you want his participation in bringing up your daughter. Don't pretend you are incompetent, but help him understand the importance of his role.
5. Include him in some of your intimate conversations with your daughter—if she agrees—so he begins to understand her thinking.
6. Remind him about her special events.
7. Laugh with him over some of her volatile adolescent behavior.
8. Love them both.

6

"*You won't let me do anything.*"

MOTHER'S LIMITS AND DAUGHTER'S DEMANDS

The Schaefer circle
In the middle: democratic parenting
Beyond the circle: decisive parenting
Applying the style to everyday issues • Follow-up
Memos for moms

"I find myself wanting to lock her in her room until she is twenty-one—and she's only fifteen," said a mother. The other mothers in the group burst out laughing in recognition of similar feelings (and fears) now that their daughters are full-blown adolescents. Many mothers secretly hope their daughters will just stay at home where they are safe until they become adults. This is especially so when a mother wakes up in the dead of night and discovers her daughter is not in her bed.

Mothers of ten- and eleven-year-old girls, on the cutting edge of adolescence, are still calm when they describe their change in attitudes: "I treat her more like an adult." "I've become more tolerant, give her more time alone, more chance to make decisions and disagree."

But mothers of older teenagers struggle to describe their changed perspective: "I'm more defensive and less patient. She tells me I don't know anything and that I'm very conservative and old-fashioned." "She is much more independent now. While I try to listen to her views more, it's tough since we disagree on so many issues."

Passage to adolescence launches a battle for territorial privileges; positions and feelings do change. Which decisions belong to mother? And which to daughter? A daughter wonders how far she can push her mother's limits and a mother wonders how much pushing she should tolerate.

Every family has its own style of making demands, meeting needs, and expressing love of their children, but as children grow older, families need to adjust their style to suit the changes in the child.

The Schaefer circle[1]

Researchers have identified various styles of parenting. The model we employ in my workshops to discuss parenting suited to adolescents was developed by Earl S. Schaefer[2] of the University of North Carolina and has been used in hundreds of research studies.

A mother may locate herself in more than one style of parenting; she may be firm on some issues and more lax on others. Or she may recognize herself in several parts of the model during her different years of parenting. Sometimes, much to her surprise, a woman may find herself in her own mother's sphere, repeating her mother's words and inflections, in spite of determined efforts to parent her daughter differently.

So readers can more easily place themselves in the Schaefer model—actually a circle of parenting styles—I am including the model. I will describe in detail each section of the circle. Many women have enjoyed discussing the circle with their husbands or their daughter's stepfather, so each can become aware of how they are reacting to their adolescent daughter.

The Schaefer circle

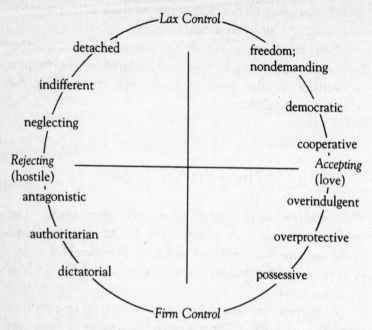

The circle is divided into four quadrants representing major dimensions of parenting behavior: *accepting* and its opposite, *rejecting*; *lax control* and its opposite, *firm control*. Both accepting and rejecting mothers may be either lax or firm in their control. There are varying degrees of control in each quadrant. A mother may recognize her own style.

LAX CONTROL

Accepting/nondemanding parenting

In the *lax control* upper half of the Schaefer circle is a nondemanding parenting style. Because a mother may love her daughter and engage in this parenting style, it is situated on the *accepting* side of the circle.

The nondemanding mother doesn't require much from her daughter, allowing her to make all her own decisions. Although most parents would deny this laid-back attitude, claiming it describes the parents of the seventies, I found during my interviews a surprising number of adolescents who felt no demands or expectations from their mothers. The girls' opinions outweigh the adults' opinions, and the mothers seem to believe that an adolescent benefits from unrestricted freedom. Some mothers, in fact, think that acceptance without demands is unconditional love. It may be unconditional, but it is not love.

One mother, described by her daughter as a "modern" parent, offers a good example of the nondemanding parent. When her daughter complained about doing something, her mother, who loved her, understood and excused her. She could be talked into anything, according to her daughter, even if it meant believing her excuses for getting into trouble or for supplying beer for parties.

From age fourteen, this girl could go where she wanted and to any hour. Of course, when it got late there was no one to hang around with, so she came home—sometimes. She admits today that she abused her freedom. "I was hanging out with the wrong people and I got into a lot of trouble. I drank and smoked pot and she never knew how deep I was getting."

Now from her perspective as a senior in high school, this daughter expresses her rage.

"My mother never preached to me about anything. She didn't talk to me about where I was going, what I was doing. She let me do whatever I wanted to do. She wouldn't make me go to school or get good grades. I would stay home and sleep and she'd make excuses for me when school called.

"I didn't care then, but now I wish she had said something. There are so many things that I wish she had done that she never did. Now I'm totally mixed up."

Her mother is trying to "crack down" on her now and it's

too late. "It's hard to learn now," she moans. "It would be so much easier if we had had rules back then, when I was in junior high." The girl left home after a fight with her mother and now lives with a friend.

What a mistake to think that caving in to a daughter's demands and not making any demands of one's own show motherly love. Loving an adolescent daughter does *not* mean letting her go.

Rejecting/detached parenting

Again, in the *lax control* half of the parenting circle, but situated on the *rejecting* side, is a neglecting, indifferent, or detached style of parenting that also grants a girl limitless freedom. A girl has freedom, in this case, not because a mother thinks this is the best way to parent but because she is too busy, has too many problems herself, or doesn't like her daughter. She seldom spends time with her daughter, doesn't share activities, and is constantly complaining or getting cross with her. Whenever the daughter wants to do something, she just plunges ahead and does it, without her mother's knowledge or advice. She knows her mother doesn't care.

Rules may be made without any thought given to the adolescent's feelings, but when they're broken, nobody notices. Mother herself may come in late, so she never observes her daughter's condition when she comes home from a party.

"My mother let me do anything," recalled a girl residing in a temporary shelter. "I used to look for ways to get into trouble just to see if she cared. There were things I did that I should have been knocked in the head for. If she had done that, I would have understood. I would not have hated her for it, but *I hate her for not disciplining me*, because that's the one thing I needed and I know I needed it."

Because her real family was so detached from her, this girl sought a substitute. "I got my family from television," she told me. "I loved 'Little House on the Prairie' and 'The Brady Bunch.' I used to be up until four or five in the morning watching those old 'I Love Lucy' shows."

Her goal today is to go into the military service "to get discipline." She has tried everything, she said as tears welled up in her eyes, to bring order into her life and nothing has succeeded. She doesn't want to see her mother again, and sadly, she doesn't believe her mother will care.

FIRM CONTROL

Accepting with control

Mothers who firmly control their teenagers are on the opposite pole from the nondemanding or detached parents. *Firm control* of an adolescent girl may seem to be a sensible way of parenting in this day of high crime and promiscuity, but on close examination this parenting style leaves a girl unprepared for life outside the home and can build resentment.

Control in the *accepting* quadrant is usually practiced by a concerned mother. In one case, a mother may subtly work on her daughter's guilt feelings to keep her daughter close, leaving a girl to wonder what she is doing that is so disturbing. A mother may inform her daughter that *if she loved her* she wouldn't have that certain group of friends, or she wouldn't choose to go to a friend's house rather than staying home. And if she *really* loved her, she would clean her room and do what she is told without arguing all the time, an adolescent pastime. A hurt tone of voice can convey an attitude of "How can you do this to me, your mother?" A daughter who should be developing her own interests and personality spends valuable time trying to figure out how to please her mother. In reality, her mother wants her to remain a child.

In another case, a girl is confused by inconsistent discipline, never knowing what to expect from her mother and not able to get clear messages from which to build her sense of self. She tiptoes around her mother's bad moods.

"My mom's like a Gemini," reported one girl, referring to the astrological sign. "A split personality. She is nice to me one minute and then the next minute tells me I'm grounded. She does this *every day*. She'll tell me she doesn't want to see me, and then five minutes later she'll be totally fine and come down and talk to my friends. I don't understand how she can change so much."

When I asked her what she would like to say to her mother, she replied, "You're giving me all these mixed messages. I wish you'd be only one person—always."

In a third example of this type of control, a mother wants to know everything her daughter does, an intrusive form of parenting that can lead to a daughter's inability to form a life outside of her mother. Her mother wants her daughter to tell her the details of what happened when she was away from home. She complains that her daughter never tells her anything. Although a mother may do this out of natural curiosity, her daughter gets the impression that she must "show and tell" throughout her adolescence and into adulthood to make her mother happy. It is not a very good way to develop a sense of oneself.

Often women recall their own mothers' methods of control during their adolescence and they don't want to repeat them. They agree with the experts that emotional control may work for a short time in reining in a daughter, but in the long run, it undermines an honest relationship and a girl's developing autonomy.

Rejecting with control

Looking again at the Schaefer circle, one can see that *firm control* can be exhibited not only by *accepting* parents but also through verbal or physical means by *rejecting* parents.

Verbal barbs and insults from a mother can devastate a girl. It can even stop her from seeking friendship because she thinks no one could possibly like someone with all her bad qualities. So she stays close to home, controlled by a destructive force. Or she rebels and finds a group suffering from similar self-hatred.

If a teenager hears constant complaining, anger, irritation, and impatience from her mother, she inevitably feels that her mother doesn't like her, even if she tries hard to do what mother wants.

"She's always saying I'm stupid," said one girl I interviewed. "I can't do anything right. I'm lazy. You know those words have an effect. They hurt a lot."

She tries to please her mother, but her mother always wants better behavior, better grades, and better looks. Nothing she does makes her mother admire her, but she keeps aspiring to be what her mother wants.

Parents who are authoritarian fall into this division of firm, hostile control. If a mother—or often a father—sets up endless rules that are inappropriate for an adolescent and enforces severe punishments for any infractions of the rules, a daughter interprets this harsh, unyielding treatment as a rejection and a denial of her individuality. She is living under a dictatorship.

Verbal attacks as a means to control a girl are destructive enough, but physical force used to control a teenager is more damaging to her development.

To see such untapped beauty and potential in girls who were beaten by their mothers, or their fathers, and to hear their tales of brutality is emotionally exhausting. These teenagers think they are real burdens to their mothers, and when asked why they think that, their responses include vivid recollections of mistreatment. A gentle, soft-spoken girl described the mistreatment she suffered from a mother who used force to control her, the mildest, in fact, of all that I heard.

"I get slapped all the time. You know, that's embarrassing. I'd get slapped in public when I was a little kid. I *really* get slapped now at home. But I'd rather have my mother beat me half to death than hear her tell me again that I'm nothing and that I'm never going to be anything if I don't do what she says."

This girl tried to get her mother to join her in counseling, but the suggestion only increased her mother's fury. I heard stories of burnings, of heavy items being thrown, and other sadistic treatments. Physical beatings occur in all segments of our supposedly "child-centered" country.

An attractive, sophisticated, well-educated woman once told me that when her thirteen-year-old daughter got "out of control" she took "a belt to her." Then, after a while, her daughter would come out of her room, apologetic and calm. I asked this mother if that was how she wanted her daughter to relate to others throughout her life—to be furious and demanding until someone, probably her husband, beat her to calm her down. It shocked this woman to think that her treatment of her daughter might lead to lifelong patterns. To her credit, she stopped beating her daughter that day and has frequently told me how grateful she is for that insight into her behavior.

How can a girl believe that her parents care for her if she is being physically attacked? Control of an adolescent girl through slapping or beating is totally inappropriate.

TOTAL IMMERSION

Overprotective or possessive parenting

Swinging back to the *accepting* side of the Schaefer circle, we see a parenting style inclining toward firm *control*. This style describes many mothers of daughters. In studies conducted by Christine Ziegler and Jerome Dusek of Syracuse University, mothers were perceived by their daughters as both *accepting and controlling*. These overprotective or possessive mothers, according to Ziegler and Dusek, foster dependency and other "traditionally feminine traits."[3]

An overinvolved mother of a teenager probably was appropriately involved during her daughter's early years but continued this total immersion into her daughter's adolescence. A mother of a little girl can love her daughter so deeply that her life revolves around her. And when her daughter reaches adolescence and is now a young woman, her mother wants to spend more time with her, aches to be included with her friends and in her school activities, wants to help her plan her social life and protect her from disappointments. She can take such pleasure in her daughter that she overidentifies with her. This loving albeit domineering mother is bound to be disappointed when her daughter begins to reject her mother's choices and doesn't want to be "protected."

A mother I know talked constantly about how wonderful her daughter's boyfriend was and could not understand why her daughter chose to break up with him. She has tried to cajole her daughter into liking him again. She thinks he is ideal for her daughter, but her daughter has other ideas.

Another girl described her mother this way: "She's really caring, almost too much so because she tends to get too involved and wants to do things for me and my sister. It kind of holds us back. For example, she keeps suggesting that we have a party or have some friends over. She thinks she's a bad mother because she can't make us happy all the time."

A teenage girl likes to take pride in her own choices, whether picking courses, boyfriends, sports, or something as trivial as the decor of her room.

"One summer in junior high I went away for a whole month and when I came home, my room was redecorated in pink and white stripes," said a girl who is now a junior in high school. "I said, sarcastically, 'Oh, how pretty,' and my mother replied, 'Your floral pillows are coming next week.' I liked my room before. Now I have this weird room. She loves it and is always making it nicer and I feel really bad. She says it's the kind of room she always wanted when she was a young girl."

When a mother seizes control of the planning and execution of a shared activity, she possesses it and her daughter will become a bystander or reluctant participant.

I have observed mothers of young horseback riders undertaking the major work in the selection, preparation, training, scheduling, and transportation of horse and rider. Usually a girl is capable of making arrangements herself. It is a good experience for her. When a mother usurps those responsibilities, she denies her daughter an opportunity for developing practical skills. If a judge scores her daughter poorly, the overinvolved mother reacts as if she herself were the rider, criticizing the judge's lack of eyesight or blaming the horse. All her daughter wants is a hug and a reassurance that her mother is proud of her participation in a competitive event.

This scenario can take place in any arena—athletic, academic, or social—when a mother is caught up in her daughter's life. This type of parenting is detrimental to a daughter, because it builds unhealthy dependency and handicaps a girl's ability to execute anything on her own.

Carried to an extreme, her daughter may rebel and reject

activities that involve her mother, perhaps turning her back on things she loves. A girl wants her mother to enjoy and share her activities, but not possess them.

In the middle: democratic parenting

In the center of the *accepting* half of the circle and halfway between lax control and firm control is democratic parenting. Some parents equate democratic parenting with permissiveness, but the two styles are not alike. When a parent is permissive, the girl's decision-making power outweighs the parent's, no matter how displeasing the decision is to her mother.

In democratic parenting, an adolescent girl is encouraged to join in on any discussion concerning her activities, to disagree with the status quo, to argue and debate, *but* the final decision must meet with her mother's approval. The give-and-take discussion before a decision is made is more appropriate for adolescents than a nondiscussed, top-down decision.

Two girls expressed the mother's role perfectly when we were discussing rule-making. "You should be open," one said, "but you can't let the kid run wild. Mothers have to have the final say." And her sixteen-year-old friend agreed: "You don't want the experimenting to go too far."

A daughter who influences her parents' opinions about curfews, parties, school expectations, and extracurricular activities is more likely to accept her family's decisions about social limits. She also knows, because her viewpoints are heard, that her mother is accepting her as an individual. Parenting becomes a two-way street, with the mother and the adolescent both accepting responsibility for the latter's behavior.

Democratic parenting is a suitable style for families with

adolescents, for it fosters competence by letting the girls know their parents depend on them to be responsible and trustworthy.

Beyond the circle: decisive parenting

Diana Baumrind's concept of "authoritative parenting"[4] was not considered in the Schaefer circle, but it is currently being discussed by psychologists concerned with increased risk-taking behavior of adolescents. In the Schaefer circle, it would fall beneath "democratic" parenting, inclining more toward firm control.

Baumrind, a well-known researcher from the University of California, Berkeley, reintroduced authority into parenting, a concept that was woefully out of fashion during the seventies. Mothers and fathers who act out of their authority as parents set high standards for their children's behavior and expect adherence to family values, which they articulate to their children. At the same time they are *"loving, supportive and committed."* They not only provide a stimulating environment for their children and encourage their teenager's independence, but also stress that family members depend on one another.

This type of parenting is not to be confused with authoritarian parenting, where the child's emerging self is ignored and all restrictions are imposed from above. Because of the possible confusion, I prefer to use the word *decisive* when referring to Baumrind's parenting style.

Baumrind's work, which followed families for a twenty-year period, has gained increased acceptance as social scientists struggle to figure out what went wrong in families in which children have serious problems. Baumrind is discovering that parents who demand responsible behavior from their children and yet remain highly responsive to their children's needs "*consistently* generated competence and deterred problem behavior in both boys and girls at *all* developmental stages."[5] Both democratic parenting (which, in Baumrind's findings, developed competent and more creative risk-taking children) and decisive parenting styles are appropriate for parents who want their adolescents to develop responsibly.

Applying the style to everyday issues

Everyday issues are magnified during adolescence, and families who do not adjust to their daughters' new demands by practicing democratic or decisive parenting find themselves entangled in petty disputes that never seem to disappear. College girls who were interviewed by researchers Grayson Holmbeck and John Hill recalled fighting with their mothers about sixteen times a month during early adolescence.[6]

CURFEWS

The debate about curfews is hottest in families with young adolescents. Most older girls think the request to be home by a specific time is reasonable—if they have had input into the decision—but twelve- to fifteen-year-olds think almost any time limitation is restrictive. Negotiating a time makes curfews less of a problem.

"I sort of stayed out too late one night in junior high," reported a high school girl. "My mother and father and I had a long talk and we agreed on a fairly decent curfew. I could understand their concern."

Another girl, who had come to appreciate her mother's patience and guidance, said, "I don't know what happened when I was twelve. I was the biggest brat and I never wanted a curfew. I was horrible. I still get that way sometimes. Recently though, my mom and I got to be really good friends. I don't know, my mom's still like a mom, she tells me what to do, but we have good times together."

Even though she fought against curfews and restrictions when she was younger, she now knows her mother was correct not to capitulate to her demands and understands that mothers have the right to tell their daughters "what to do."

Parent and community groups can be helpful in suggesting curfew guidelines. Parent-Teacher Associations often publish party guidelines that are sent to families in a school district. When families in an area agree on recommended curfews, life is easier for mothers and gives them ammunition against the old ploy of "Everyone else does it."

THE BEDROOM

The bedroom can be a last battleground for territorial rights. It is always a mess, no matter how recently it has been cleaned. Patient mothers close the door and save their ammunition for more important matters, but some mothers cannot tolerate the chaos.

That lack of tolerance can have an angry effect on girls who are performing well in other arenas. One girl, an overachiever in all her activities, talked about cleaning her room.

"Not cleaning my room—that's always the big thing. I just get home from play practice. I haven't eaten since noon and it's nine or nine-thirty at night. I'm so tired I'm ready to pass out and she wants me to clean my room. I have three tests to study for and she wants me to clean. I don't have time for this and cleaning my room is about as important as clipping my toenails."

Over and over again, messy bedrooms crept into my conversations with girls whose lives were otherwise in order. One girl summed it up when she said, "We're basically normal kids and they have to find something that's wrong and the room is the thing.

"My room's not bad," she continued. "My brother's room smells. The stench would knock you over, but they don't complain to him because I'm the perfectionist. If she complains to me, I feel real bad. My brother just ignores it."

If a sloppy room really bothers a mother, then she has to sit down with her daughter and figure out ways to remove it as a source of friction. The girl's ideas must be included in the solution. Most girls will agree to arrange a time each week to attack the mess, but it should be their choice of when.

If there are times when a mother cannot wait—if she is expecting guests, for example—she should request a clean room in a calm and reasonable voice. Most girls respond to polite requests. If sisters share a room, then the two of them should work out an arrangement to their own satisfaction.

There is something to be said for perspective. After six children, I have learned what is important and what is secondary to me. Not only is a tidy room a low priority, but I am amazed at the order that exists in the chaos. My youngest knows exactly where everything is, which pile has the cleanest or dirtiest clothes, and where the scrap of paper with an important number is. It is her territory and, thankfully, we do not need to use her room frequently.

Follow-up

A democratic or decisive mother who is confident about her values, committed and responsive to her adolescent, and trusts her daughter while being vigilant to signs of trouble creates an environment in which the adolescent can flourish. This type of parenting, however, does not end when the decisions are agreed upon; it continues into being aware of a daughter's attitudes and choices.

In studies of high school youth, Sanford Dornbusch of Stanford University found that these students were likely to make value choices that were approved by their peers rather than their parents. However, when it came to acting on those choices, a good majority of the students said that if their friends' views differed from their parents' views, they would choose the standards of their parents. The adolescents would follow their parents' values *if* they thought their parents would find out about it.[7] In other words, if a mother is vigilant and aware of her adolescent's activities, the girl will be more inclined to choose her mother's values. What Dornbusch calls "parental monitoring" I call "vigilant trust."

"Mothers shouldn't impose a lot of restrictions," said a girl who spoke fondly about her mother. "That won't be too good. And if they're totally open, that won't be good. My mother's not lax. She's not strict. She's somewhere in between. We agree about a lot of things and she always looks at my point of view. I love my mom. I like her a lot."

MEMOS FOR MOMS

1. Encourage your daughter's participation in decisions that affect her, listen to her ideas, and be willing to follow them, but keep in mind that you have the final approval.

2. Remember that giving her complete freedom is *not* what she wants. She needs to remain connected to the family.

3. Let her know your values and your expectations for her behavior.

4. Make sure she is aware of your commitment to her and your affection for her.

5. Pay attention to her activities and know her friends.

6. Keep up your own interests so your psyche is not dependent on her successes or failures.

7. Show flexibility. Make exceptions to family rules for special occasions.

8. Have confidence in yourself as a parent. It gives her strength.

9. Be direct and honest in your comments. Do not use sarcasm or insults.

10. Never use physical punishment or coercion.

11. Don't argue over trivial issues. Agree on which areas are her domain and responsibility and stick to that agreement.

12. Include her in family decisions and activities, so she realizes that family members depend on one another.

7

"I'm too fat. Look at my thighs."

A WOMAN'S BODY: NEVER GOOD ENOUGH

Causes • Culture's demands • Body image
The family • Voices • Trying to please • Discovery
Signs of anorexia nervosa • Signs of bulimia
Treatment • Amy's story • Memos for moms

❦ Our culture worships thin thighs, the athletic look, and food. What a bind for the adolescent girl, absorbed as she is with her appearance!

On the one hand, she is surrounded by fast foods, high-calorie snacks, low-calorie soft drinks (which increase appetite), ice cream and cookie parlors, and junk-food palaces. On the other hand, society and teen magazines persistently bombard her with the diet message: lose weight, get thin, and you'll be happy. Or if you're unhappy, lose weight and then you'll have no problems.

Some teens succumb to the lure of high-calorie food, then react to the "thin means happy" message with relentless dieting. Other girls are driven to binge and then purge themselves of the hated calories by vomiting or using laxatives. Still others try to maintain pseudo control over their bodies by not eating at all.

These ways of trying to control body weight, either by gorging and purging (bulimia) or by starving (anorexia nervosa), constitute a serious threat to a girl's mental and physical health and to her family's equilibrium.

The quandary is, why do some girls develop these eating disorders while other girls remain immune? Can mothers spot vulnerable girls early enough to help them avoid these food obsessions?

Causes

If we could only define the causes of eating disorders, solutions might be easy. But the causes, the precise origins, remain unknown. Researchers are suggesting that multiple factors, not identical with each girl, contribute to the disorders.

From the work of Joan Jacobs Brumberg in her well-documented history of eating disorders, *Fasting Girls*, we do know that anorexia nervosa is not a recent phenomenon. It was described in journals of the Middle Ages and was classified in 1873 as a distinct disease affecting young, middle-class females. However, the disorder was relatively rare until about twenty years ago. Now estimates of young American women burdened with some degree of eating disorder range from 5 to 20 percent.[1]

Although eating disorders have been described as adolescent illnesses, if unresolved they continue to have a pervasive effect throughout adulthood. Women in their late thirties have told me they have been obsessed with food since their early teen years and this fixation has dominated their lives.

Many factors could turn a girl's desire for thinness into an eating disorder. Experts don't always agree, but the contributing factors could range from a family structure that inhibits emotional expression, to society's current expectations for superwomen, to developmental difficulties arising during adolescence, to serious underlying mental problems or sexual abuse of the girl.

Culture's demands

What our culture's mania for thinness says to our adolescents and to women in general is that a woman's body with generous hips, full breasts, and soft muscles must be transformed into small hips, flat chests, and discreet firm muscles. *Most adolescents afflicted with an eating disorder have launched the alteration of their bodies with a diet they have read about or their mother or a friend has suggested.*

Magazines for teenage girls (and women), rather than stressing the merits of intellectual, artistic, creative, or social development, accentuate the body by lauding the prepubescent look of a model's body, promoting diets for girls who, in fact, need body fat to become women.

Brumberg suggests that adolescent girls in our culture also are likely to have "anxiety over their sexuality and the implications of changing sex roles." At a time when a girl is preoccupied with her developing body, she observes changing standards of male-female interactions in her family, and she doesn't possess the maturity to establish her own feelings about the new relationships. The cultural norms for her are in a state of flux. She vacillates between wanting a "woman's role" or a "man's role" and is too young to find her own niche. One solution is to turn to starvation to avoid sexual resolutions, to become asexual.

Not knowing how to interact with boys also may cause a girl to want to resort to a child's body. Being anorexic pushes away the demands of becoming a woman, of being independent and facing adulthood.

Body image

Jeanne Brooks-Gunn studied ways to identify eating problems that have the potential to escalate into clinical eating disorders. With Ilana Attie from Cornell Medical Center, Brooks-Gunn followed a group of normal girls from middle school to high school to see if eating problems developed as a response to puberty.

She found that in an early-adolescent population, rapid accumulation of body fat *coupled with a poor body image* may predispose an adolescent to eating problems in middle or late adolescence. The girls Brooks-Gunn questioned were normal-weight adolescents, yet many complained about how fat they were.

When the girls reached age sixteen and were questioned again by the researchers, those with negative feelings about their bodies and themselves when they were in middle school were more likely to have developed eating disorders.[2]

In a study that looked at adolescent values, Joseph Allen and his colleagues at Yale University found that when an adolescent girl diets to stay *very* thin, she thinks she is pleasing adults. Eighty-two percent of the seventh and eighth graders they interviewed responded that adults place *high value* on the idea that "a girl diets to stay very thin."[3]

The prevalence of young women with poor body images and eating problems can become almost epidemic in a college population. In a study of 643 *normal* (not clinically anorexic or obese) college women, Laurie Mintz and Nancy Betz of Ohio State University found that a scant 33 percent reported normal eating habits. While only 3 percent could be classified as bulimic, 61 percent exhibited some form of eating problem such as chronic dieting (with or without pills and laxatives) or binge-eating and deliberate purging, but not frequently enough to be labeled bulimic.

This study of women in one college also found that the degree of eating problems was strongly associated with negative body image, belief in female thinness, lowered self-esteem, and obsessive thoughts about weight and appearance.[4]

Negative body images that lead to eating disorders begin to develop during early adolescence, so now is the time for a mother to be aware of her daughter's feelings about herself and her body.

The family

A group of anorexic and bulimic teenage girls were gathered in an intimate room for interviews with me. The session was part of ongoing therapy, so the girls knew one another. Their lack of emotion was startling and in stark contrast to the girls without eating disorders whom I met in school settings and who immediately opened up and talked about their mothers with animation, humor, love, and hatred.

When the girls with eating disorders were asked the same questions about their mothers, there was dead silence. Their silence revealed the defenses they use to distance themselves from their feelings. Halfway through the session, a few girls, those who seemed the most advanced in the recovery program, began to talk about their relationships with their mothers.

Popular books, especially those by Kim Chernin, propose that eating disorders stem from the entanglement of mothers and daughters, that emotions stifled by mothers are expressed through food.[5] Although some evidence does exist to support this psychoanalytical theory, I think the disorder is far more complex. Research is inconclusive, so rather than attempt an analysis of the family structure of a problem eater, I will let the girls speak for themselves.

One pattern of mother-daughter interaction did emerge from our discussions. Many of the girls' mothers were themselves heavily involved in dieting, were concerned with food, or talked a lot about staying thin. The boundaries between the girls and their mothers were blurry. It seemed as though the mothers considered their bodies and their daughters' bodies as one, without distinguishing their separateness.

It is necessary to distinguish further between anorexia nervosa and bulimia. An anorexic girl is starving herself, and her loss of weight will become apparent to an observant mother. She also may initiate frenetic exercise and she will stop having periods. Even if she wears oversize clothes, her weight loss eventually can be noticed.

A bulimic girl may not be noticed as easily because her weight loss may not be as dramatic and she will binge and vomit outside of her family's surveillance. Also, a girl will often combine anorexic and bulimic behavior—that is, she will starve herself for a length of time, then binge and then purge. However, most bulimic girls do leave traces of their behavior, clues that can be picked up by vigilant families. I will discuss all the signs of eating disorders further in this chapter.

Voices

The voices throughout this chapter of girls with eating disorders are those of young women emerging, with the help of therapy, into a sense of themselves. Their struggles with food are terrifying, dominating their days and nights. I hope that, by listening to their experiences, mothers will feel more capable of leading their daughters away from the path of eating problems.

"I think a lot of my ideas came from my mother," commented a very quiet, beautiful sophomore. "My family is split in half. My dad eats well. Mom and I used to eat together. We were always on diets and then we'd go off them together. We'd eat tons of ice cream sitting around the kitchen counter."

"The things she criticized in me were the things she saw in herself," said a college girl who has been bulimic since early junior high days. "Especially when she herself became real thin, she used to tease me about being fat, and I was very thin. She used to tease me all the time. She used to single me out. I have a brother and sister, but she didn't tease them."

"My mom's kind of hard to deal with," admitted a high school girl struggling to find the right words. "I overidentify with her. She was anorexic when I was in junior high school."

These girls reinforced my belief that, during early adolescence, food should be a *nondiscussable issue*. If mothers are concerned with their own weight, they should not talk about it. They should keep fresh, healthy food readily available in the house, serve well-balanced meals, and then forget about what the girls eat outside of the house. No one has died from eating junk food, but girls have died from self-inflicted starvation.

One mother told me she took her twelve-year-old to a diet center because she was five to ten pounds overweight. It is all right for a girl to be overweight, I assured her. I prefer seeing an overweight adolescent than an underweight one. Another mother whose daughter was hospitalized with anorexia nervosa said she would innocently ask her daughter, "How many calories in that yogurt?" She was always watching her daughter's intake. Her daughter was a slip of a thing and did not have a weight problem, although she thought she was fat.

I think mothers could help girls avoid eating disorders if

they dealt only with their own bodies and let their daughters deal with their own bodies. In other words, keep the boundaries between them clearly defined.

Trying to please

Often the girl who becomes anorexic or bulimic has been a model child, a good student, compliant and helpful. On the outside, she may appear perfect, but she hides self-doubts as she tries hard to please her mother.

"My mom is a perfectionist. She never compliments me," a girl who has been in treatment for a long time quietly remarked. "She had a real rough childhood. She took responsibility for being a mother to her mother and being a mother to her younger brother and sister. She tries to do everything for me. I don't think she understands why she does things, but she's very good at convincing herself that she does the right thing under any circumstance. I'm easily persuaded by her because she gives the impression that she can never be wrong."

When I asked her what she would like to say to her mother, she replied, "Be able to admit that you're wrong, that you have faults. Don't try to be so strong all the time. Don't try to be invincible."

Another girl said that after some therapy, her family discovered that they "were putting some kind of social pressure on me to succeed and be very friendly, to be perfect. Everyone always knew that I was the shy one and didn't talk. That was my nature and nothing could be changed no matter how hard they tried and I tried."

These girls demand a lot of themselves and need a relaxed home where everyone makes mistakes and family members come in assorted shapes with distinct, dissimilar personalities.

The adage "variety is the spice of life" will convey a message of acceptance to girls who think perfection is the only acceptable standard.

Discovery

Discovering if a girl is anorexic or bulimic may require very attentive parenting, but as one of the girls told me, "Only three percent of girls who come in here for treatment are diagnosed as nonanorexic. So if mothers are suspicious they should go for help. Mothers should trust their sense."

Curious about how these girls' eating disorders were detected, I asked if they would share that experience with other mothers.

"I started dieting in the seventh grade," said one girl. "In November of my junior year in high school, I said to my mother that I thought I was anorexic and she denied it emphatically. I had been throwing up since my freshman year so she was denying it for a long time. There were so many obvious signs. I'd leave throw-up around. I didn't know at the time I was doing it. When the doctor confirmed that I had a problem, she got really mad at me for weeks. She was disappointed in me. I was the perfect child. She was disappointed in herself because she wasn't the perfect mother."

"My mom was just really scared," said another girl whose mother suspected a disorder but was afraid to act. "When I finally did go to a doctor, she said she suspected it a long time ago and wished she had done something about it. She was taking books from the library for eight months before I went into the hospital. She had always read a whole bunch of psychology books and I guess when she began noticing I was becoming more preoccupied with food, she began looking into it. She practically accused me of having problems, but she didn't ask me a lot of questions and I was trying anything I could to worm out of the doctor's appointments."

One girl told me that she left signs all over, but they were not detected. For instance, the toilet had to be repaired ten times during her unnoticed bulimic stage. No one associated a clogged toilet with an eating disorder, but she knew what was happening.

Other girls said they never ate in front of their parents, always claiming they had just eaten at a friend's house, certainly a strange phenomenon for a normal teenager. Some took dinner to their room "to study" and disposed of it.

When one of the girls I interviewed said her mother did not know about her eating disorder until she told her, I believed her. It is possible that she was clever enough to conceal it completely by never being seen without wearing bulky clothes.

If a mother notices any of the behaviors or signs mentioned above, she must act immediately because her daughter may be suffering from an eating disorder. Mothers are usually the first ones to detect if a child is not feeling well or behaving differently. They should trust their hunches and go to a doctor. Some communities are fortunate enough to have an eating-disorder clinic nearby, where a mother can go for a consultation with or without her daughter. If a clinic is not available, the pediatrician should be able to recommend a specialist. The quicker a disorder is diagnosed, the more likely a girl will be able to return to a normal life.

Signs of anorexia nervosa

Since most diets are not successful, a daughter who is successfully dieting bears watching. Dieters usually are sociable about their dieting, according to Dr. Diane Mickley, director of the Wilkins Center for Eating Disorders, but anorexics are not. They are protective and secretive. Dr. Mickley recommends being direct with a girl: "Lay the cards on the table." If a daughter protests vigorously, denying anything out of the ordinary with her eating, but a mother suspects differently, she should go with her suspicion and seek help immediately.[6]

The signs of anorexic behavior can be detected. If a girl's menstrual periods stop, it could be caused by irregular periods common in puberty, by extensive exercise, or by starvation. This sign of an eating disorder may appear before the weight loss. A doctor should check it out. A mother must make sure her daughter keeps the appointment.

Another obvious indication of anorexia is severe loss of weight. A girl must lose 15 percent of her body weight, or not gain weight as she grows, to be clinically diagnosed an anorexic, but by then her starvation or her binge-eating and purging may have become an entrenched habit. If she is showing an unexplained loss of weight or not gaining normal weight, she must see a doctor.

Often anorexic girls will become hyperactive, engaging in strenuous and prolonged exercise. One girl told me she rode her stationary bike for hours, *after* she had returned from field hockey practice.

An anorexic girl will become preoccupied with food and weight. She may begin preparing large meals for the family, but she will not touch them herself. She may talk a lot about food and diets and how food smells and looks.

She may develop a covering of fine hair over her body, but begin to lose some of the hair on her head.

A mother may become conscious of a change in her daughter's attitudes, an unexplained loss of interest in many activities, a depression that lasts longer than the typical adolescent mood swing, and an extreme dissatisfaction with her body.

Signs of bulimia

If a girl is binge-eating and purging but not manifesting severe weight loss, uncovering it may be more difficult. Bulimia is called the "secret disease" because girls—and women—become very adroit at concealing the evidence.

Food may disappear without explanation. A mother may find herself constantly shopping and then wondering where all the groceries have gone, not realizing that her daughter is stashing food in her room, in the cupboards, or in the garage in order to gorge herself in private. It pays to be aware of that possibility.

The girl's periods become very irregular. They may not stop completely, but they will become abnormally irregular as her weight fluctuates.

The acid from the extensive vomiting will cause her teeth to lose their enamel, leading to tooth decay.

Treatment

A surprising number of girls are knowledgeable about the life-threatening effects of anorexia and bulimia, but they continue to starve or binge and purge because they have lost control. Ironically, a girl may initiate a diet to gain control of herself, but then obsession with food controls her.

When her condition is serious enough for her to enter treatment, all factors influencing her young life—societal, psychological, and biological—have to be examined. Therapy must treat all elements of the disorder

Through support groups, the societal and cultural expectations of contemporary women can be addressed. In these groups, fears about gaining weight or surviving in a competitive world are aired as the girls learn to disassociate being skinny and being successful.

Psychological therapy is essential in reestablishing a girl's self-image and sense of effectiveness. Psychiatrist Gerald Russell and his associates from Royal Free Hospital, London, have found family therapy to be most successful with patients whose disorder had lasted less than three years before treatment and had begun before they were eighteen.[7] Individual therapy is also critical, according to Dr. Diane Mickley, and should be long-term to be most effective.[8]

Most treatment centers employ nutritionists who teach girls good eating habits and help bring them up to normal weight. This nutritional information is an essential component of recovery, reassuring the girls that eating healthy food does not mean getting fat.

Girls in treatment certainly need good medical care on all levels to replace the vitamins and minerals purged from their systems and to have support in monitoring their physical recovery. Some physicians are finding tentative success in treating bulimia with drug therapy as part of the complete therapeutic program.

Some girls may require hospitalization; their stays vary from one month to a year. Mothers should not hesitate to inquire if their daughters need this intensive treatment in an adolescent unit. The time to resolve the problem is when a girl is young; don't let it linger into adult life. It shows true motherly concern and love to act immediately, and a daughter will appreciate it after she has recovered.

Awareness of the problem has led to the creation of eating-disorder self-help groups around the country. The establishment of the American Anorexia/Bulimia Association (418 E. 76 St., New York, N.Y. 10021 (212) 734-1114) by parents of anorexic/bulimic victims has been welcomed by all families affected by this illness. The association puts out a newsletter and various other publications.

Amy's story

Amy is a good-looking, enthusiastic, healthy senior in high school who has successfully recovered from anorexic bulimia. This is her story.

"I started out with just a diet. Then I stopped eating dinner, then lunch, and then breakfast. For a period of three days I'd eat nothing and then I'd eat and throw it up. It was a combination of starving myself, eating a meal, and then panicking, throwing up, and then exercising for three hours. I started in December of tenth grade and told my parents about it in April.

"I lost thirty-five pounds. My mom loves to cook and family meals were always a big thing in my house. My mom's father died in the fall, and then in December her sister died. Starting in November, my mother was in Pennsylvania a lot taking care of her mother and my dad traveled a lot. My brother is a junk-food eater so he didn't notice.

"When my mom was home I would still get away with it. I would go to the library right at dinnertime or I would pick a fight with my mother or brother so I would be sent out of the kitchen. I had a whole bunch of little ways to get out of dinner. If my mom would bug me, I would say, 'Do you want me to eat or fail?'

"I would come home from basketball practice and ride my exercise bike for two hours, then ride the rowing machine for a half hour and do sit-ups and leg lifts in front of the television. My brother would be there eating a bowl of ice cream and he'd say, 'Would you stop that.' My mom noticed things were changing, but she was so preoccupied with her mom, she wasn't focused on me.

"Then my eating began to bother my mom and dad. When I was home at dinner, they would tell me to eat and I would panic. The more they said, the more I would be determined not to eat. I really knew what I was doing was wrong, but I had to get to a certain point before I realized how much trouble I was in. I wanted to be skinny so much that nothing would stop me.

"Before puberty I was a total twig, never showed a thing. When I started going into puberty and gained weight, I probably wasn't fat but I felt fat. I had just moved from California and left all my friends. I hated my new school. My grandfather and aunt died. Everything was out of control. I could look perfect on the outside, but I had all this pain on the inside. I thought if I looked perfect, nothing could hurt me anymore. I rationalized, but it didn't work. The deeper I got into it, the worse it got. I would study through lunch. You would look at my grades and say, 'What a student!' You would look at me and say, 'What a skinny girl! She must have everything together.'

"I didn't want to accept puberty. I didn't want anything else to hurt me. I was mad at my grandfather and my aunt for dying. I was furious that they did this to me just when we had moved back to this area and I could see them again.

"When I began doing this, I went to the library and read and read. I was totally informed. I knew why all this hair was growing over me. My skin dried out, my hair fell out, and that terrified me. My hands and knuckles were shaking. I knew I could rupture my esophagus and die. I analyzed and over-analyzed. I read things into my parents and blamed it on everyone but myself.

"I started making cookies for everyone. I loved watching my brother eat. I would show control over myself. One night I made a five-course meal. I watched them eat and then I put the leftovers in the refrigerator because I didn't want to be with food by myself.

"If people offered me food, I'd say, 'No, thank you.' I'd feel like a strong person, but by myself I would lose that control. If I lost control I would have to throw up or exercise for three hours. And it hurt, making myself throw up, very uncomfortable, emotionally as well. It made me feel so bad about myself, because it physically hurts and emotionally it makes you feel like such a failure. I would tell myself I wouldn't do this again and then I would do it again and feel like such a failure and I couldn't stop.

"I think in a way I wanted to stay my mommy's little girl. I remember at my grandfather's funeral, my mom held everyone together and was taking care of everyone and I remember I was thinking, 'Who am I left with?' I was just standing there crying by myself and I have this picture of myself always by myself.

"In the beginning of April, I was at my cousin's wedding and she took out pictures of really anorexic, sick-looking people and said, 'This is what happens to you when you're anorexic.' I was sitting there thinking, 'Why are you telling me this?' But I guess it did scare me, because I went home and said to my mom the next day, 'Mom, I have to talk to you.' "

Amy's story is typical in a number of ways. She was not willing to accept her new figure during puberty because she wanted to stay a "twig." She was experiencing dramatic changes: new school, no friends, death of two close relatives, father traveling in a new job, mother preoccupied with her widowed mother, and puberty. She wanted attention, so she sought approval through perfection in schoolwork, looks, and athletics.

Amy's story has a happy ending because her family reacted immediately and her disorder was short-lived. As soon as she found out, Amy's mother took her to a center for eating disorders, even though Amy had begged her not to tell anyone, saying that she could conquer it by herself. Her mother, however, knew that Amy needed professional help and did not hesitate. Her family cooperated with the psychologist, the doctor, and the nutritionist and did not deny there was a problem. The fact that Amy was afflicted for only six months before seeking help was a strong factor in her favor.

However, recovery was not an easy process, and both Amy and her parents had to adjust.

"It was hard on my mother. I told her that unless I mentioned my disorder, I did not want her to mention it. I said to them, 'I don't want you guys to think that every time I go into the bathroom, I'm sticking my finger down my throat.' I got really paranoid. I didn't want anyone to know about it. When I told my parents I thought they would think I was totally disgusting, and I wanted their approval, not their disgust.

"I still don't talk to my mother a lot about it because she puts a lot of the blame on herself. I wrote an essay about it and my mom read it and started crying about it. *They are so proud of me for overcoming it.*"

When I asked Amy how she felt now, she responded, "I blamed it on my mother in the beginning, but then I recognized if I wanted to be an independent person, I would have to take responsibility for myself and I did by telling my parents and going through recovery and getting myself out of it. I gained a lot of self-esteem. I'm happier now and have higher self-esteem than before it started."

As you can gather, Amy had a good sense of herself before she reached puberty. The disruption of her family life during a critical time in adolescence was more than she could handle. However, her supportive family, once they realized Amy's agony, united to help her overcome her obsession. Also, she and her mother have begun to appreciate each other's differences. For instance, Amy has become "more tolerant" of her mother's love of art, even going to a museum once in a while, and her mother is trying to learn about sports.

Amy and the other eating-disorder girls I interviewed touched me deeply. They will continue struggling with their obsession with food until they find peace with themselves and their bodies. As one girl said, "You can avoid alcohol or drugs if you're addicted to them, but you can't avoid food."

Previous generations of mothers and daughters did not have this worry about eating disorders, but the present generation of mothers of adolescent girls must take this life-threatening problem into consideration. By maintaining family environments that show love and appreciation of adolescent girls' personalities and bodies, mothers will foster normal, healthy development.

MEMOS FOR MOMS

1. Don't talk about food or diet when your daughter is an adolescent. Prepare healthy food and forget about what she eats outside the home. Food must be a nonissue.
2. Examine your own feelings about a woman's body. She picks up your verbal and nonverbal messages.
3. Be positive about her new figure.
4. Watch for signs of weight loss or overconcern with food.
5. Don't comment about her eating. ("You're not helping if you bug her about what she does or does not eat." "They talked about it so much that it made me start eating a lot and then getting rid of it.")
6. Let her express her feelings, good or bad. Listen and be sympathetic. ("When I first mentioned I was depressed, that was like a naughty word—like no, that's unthinkable, you only have good feelings.")
7. Make family meals happy times. Don't concentrate on what they're eating or on manners. Teach good manners separately.
8. Discontinue buying magazines that glorify a slim body. Show her by example that other qualities are more important than looks. ("I knew my friend had

a problem when I went to her house and she had a mural of models and skinny girls. She had a picture of a girl in a bathing suit on the refrigerator.")

9. Notice if she has her periods regularly. Cessation of periods is one of the first signs of an eating disorder.
10. Be aware of the signs of eating disorders.
11. Respect and appreciate her growing body.
12. If your school requires "skinfold tests," which measure a child's fat, urge that they be discontinued. Body fat is related to an adolescent's stage of development. Each girl has a different amount of body fat; there is no universal ideal level.
13. Respect her as an individual with her own body and personality.

8

♥

"Everyone is fighting for popularity."

THE IMPORTANCE OF FRIENDS

♥

Excluding mother
Coping with rejection • Isolation
Keeping self-esteem • Making friends • Keeping friends
Accepting her friends • Peer pressure
Memos for moms

❤️ Friends are the passport into the world of adolescence, a subculture that functions outside parental observation. To gain entrance into this world, a girl must plan her daily invasion of school carefully.

Her strategy requires the precision of a scientist. Doubts nag her: What shirt, pants, shoes should I wear? Where will I meet someone to walk in with me? Will I see anyone I know when we change class? Where will I sit during lunch? What seat should I take in math class? How can I cover up my pimples? Will they ask me if I bought my clothes at a flea market? Why can't I look like Jennifer?

By the time the adolescent has left for school, she is tense and her mother is exhausted. Fitting in is hard work during those years, but it is all-important since inclusion in the popular group means her social worries are over—or at least this is what she thinks.

When our thirteen-year-old transferred schools between seventh and eighth grades, she knew no one and worried about being accepted. I couldn't get her off my mind that first day. Had we made the right decision? Would she find friends?

Two girls came up and introduced themselves in her first class. Their simple greeting eased her stress. And I measured the success of her first day not in the brilliance of the teachers or the magnificence of the building but in that simple act of friendship. And so did she.

The girls I talked with confirmed that making friends becomes a girl's top priority during junior high years. It is hard work.

"Eighth grade was a real transition year for me as far as friends go," recalled one, now a high school junior. "You don't know who you really are and you don't know who your friends are."

A friend agreed, "It was more difficult to know where you fit in. A lot of girls were fighting over little things so problems got blown out of proportion. Seventh and eighth grade are hard times; you do a lot of growing. Everyone is fighting for popularity."

In early adolescence, girls are very conscious of their relationships, more than boys, and are sensitive to any negative evaluations from friends. And because each girl's rate of maturity is unique, she may feel out of place with her old friends. She thinks her old school friends are immature (which means they are not interested in boys), and they, in turn, may feel uncomfortable with her. She also wants to test friendships with girls from different backgrounds or different schools, girls she would not meet as family friends or in her small circle of elementary school pals. She may explore many different types of friendships until she realizes that friendships come from common interests, not from a shared maturity level.

If mothers understood just how important friends are to a teenager, they would be more likely to make an effort to understand their daughters' friends and would realize how friendships change.

Excluding mother

"My mother had a hard time realizing I wanted to be with my friends more than I wanted to be with the family," said one girl. "It's not that I hate them or anything; I just want to be with my friends."

That girl's mother needed to know that a girl will devote a lot of time to making and keeping friends. Friends require nurturing, and that's more important to a teenager than any other obligation.

Friends also experience events and feelings that cannot be shared with mothers. When the telephone cord is stretched out the length of the room and into the bathroom and the door is shut, a mother gets the distinct feeling she's being excluded. The conversation behind a closed door piques her curiosity. She tries to eavesdrop or she opens the door and asks, "What are you talking about that you can't talk about in front of me?"

"Nothing," says her daughter.

As maddening as that response is, it is the best response a teenager can make. She probably isn't talking about anything confidential, and she probably isn't talking about anything very important. But she will certainly not converse with friends in front of her mother. A mother is left with snatches of conversation, hearing incomplete information about her daughter's friends and activities.

What a change from the time she knew all her daughter's elementary school friends to this time of strange voices and unfamiliar names that she cannot connect with a face.

Teenage girls must invest energy and time on building friendships. They find out that problems arise when they neglect friends. When a girl leaves another out of her plans, ignores her, doesn't come to parties, or doesn't call, her friend will find a replacement. Mothers can help by including friends in family events and by understanding their daughters' demands to spend more time with their friends.

Coping with rejection

Robert and Beverly Cairns and their colleagues from the University of North Carolina followed a group of children from fourth through ninth grade, observing the children's aggressive behavior toward one another. There were striking differences in the behavior of boys and girls as they entered adolescence.

The boys confronted each other directly with fights and verbal assaults (a so-called brutality norm). The girls, in general, were more indirect and used manipulation to communicate hostility, sort of a clique mentality. They tended to isolate someone they disliked by spreading rumors, rejecting her from social activities, alienating her from the group, or accusing her unjustly of violating their codes of behavior.[1]

Research such as that of the Cairnses documents the experiences of girls I interviewed. They report that making friends is far more difficult in junior high than in senior high. By senior high, girls generally have found comfortable friends and the boundaries of a group are less rigid, allowing more of a flow among groups. In senior high girls appreciate one another more, but in junior high a girl is on her own.

"At my new school I became part of a group that I would have looked down on at my old school," said one girl with pain in her voice as she talked about making friends. "I would invite them over once in a while because they always invited me over and my mom would criticize them afterwards. At that time I would have liked my mom not to notice that I was not as popular as I had been. I wanted her to think I was the all-together kid she always thought I was. I was already feeling bad about myself and then she knocked my friends. It hurt."

Although this girl was not satisfied with her new friends, at least she had some. Not all girls find companionship. A mother should value her daughter's friends, even if they are not girls she herself would have chosen for her daughter. Unless there is evidence that a friend is introducing a girl into alcohol or drug use, her mother should be grateful that her daughter has someone to talk with.

Isolation

When a girl is the victim of the local class bully, the recipient of social rejection, a victim of physical aggression, or simply stood up by her supposed best friend, a mother's heart can break right along with her child's.

Mothers in my workshops tell anguishing tales. Not all of their daughters have endured the humiliation of repeated rejection, but it takes only one occurrence to devastate a girl.

A girl who was new in a school was deliberately tripped and her books knocked out of her arms as she walked up the aisle in class. The same girl was threatened when she asked a student in art class to turn down the radio.

Another, a sixteen-year-old, was left stranded at her first formal dance. Her date spent the evening working with his musician friends and paying attention to his real girlfriend, leaving this girl by herself. She even had to find her own ride home.

Then there was the humiliation of an eighth-grade girl who was stood up for the third time by a "friend" who said she would pick her up for a movie. Since this person belonged to the inner circle, the girl's abandonment became public knowledge to the whole class.

Occasionally, this mean-spirited behavior can permeate a

particular grade or classroom through the intimidation of a bullying person or group. The school staff may be oblivious to the turmoil, since most encounters take place when there is no supervision. If a girl is ostracized in such a class, I would recommend talking to her counselor. A school can conduct interpersonal skill sessions with the students. If one girl is being harassed, there are probably many more who are reluctant to reveal their unfair treatment by peers.

Keeping self-esteem

A mother's attitude takes on added importance during these years because she has a powerful impact on a girl's self-esteem. Some girls need bolstering to be able to withstand hostile treatment from classmates.

"If a girl is comfortable at home, she'll develop a good sense of herself," said one of the girls I talked to. And she added that "a sense of herself" will protect her from the distress of isolation. So as much as a mother is aware of her daughter's need to have friends outside the home, she herself may have to step in for a while to provide companionship.

A high school girl whom I would identify as bright and quiet came with a group of close friends to one of our talk sessions.

"In junior high, in all honesty, I had zero friends," she said. "I had a lot of friends once, and they all ditched me. I didn't keep one friend through junior high. My mom kept saying that it was okay, that from what she could tell I wasn't doing anything wrong. She encouraged me to keep being the person I was, not to change."

If a girl remains friendless and becomes increasingly despondent, then counseling is appropriate. The problem may lie deeper than just being left out of a social life. Maybe she is choosing to remain friendless because of feelings of inadequacy or a fear of facing the world without her family. Adolescence is the best time to uncover the causes behind unhappiness, before it turns into clinical depression. When a girl acquires a good "sense of self" through therapy and a supportive family, she will find it easier to share her life with friends and reach out beyond her family.

Making friends

Friends seem to come effortlessly to some girls and tortuously to others. If a girl is surrounded with friends, then the friend worries are few, especially if her mother likes them. But other mothers may have to help their daughters reach out.

Suggestions can only be offered; the reluctance to follow through on them must be understood. Most adults, for instance, would hesitate to telephone a person they had met briefly. When a mother suggests her daughter call a girl she would like to get to know better, her daughter's indecision is understandable. Will the recipient of her call have too many friends already to include her in any plans? When a mother says, "Why don't you ask Lisa to go to the movies with you?," her daughter may cringe at the suggestion because she fears Lisa will say she is busy and can't go.

Since breaking into an established group may be too challenging for a girl, she should be encouraged to develop her own group. A mother and daughter can look over a list of school activities such as intramural or varsity sports; language, science, art, math, drama, dance clubs; peer counseling; social concerns groups; and school service organizations. Community teen activities may center on the YWCA or Girls Club, both of which usually are looking for young members.

And young people are needed to participate on drug- and alcohol-prevention committees, in religious organizations, or in hospital volunteer programs. The local paper will give such information. The list of places is long in most communities, and a girl who joins in will find others who share her interests, a good basis for friendship.

If a girl has decided to make friends with a certain classmate, her mother can suggest ways to go about it. For instance, listen carefully when the other girl talks about her own interests, and ask questions. (How do you like the coach? Where did you find out so much about jazz? How did you get that color to come out so well?) Girls will like having friends notice what they are doing.

Also, a mother can remind her daughter that everyone likes compliments. Although a girl may think it's phony to pay a compliment, she knows how she feels when someone appreciates the good work or effort she has put into a project. By showing appreciation, offering a simple "thank you," or noticing a piece of clothing ("I like your shoelaces"), she will make the girl feel good about herself and pave the way for friendship. By putting the compliment in the first person ("I love your hair that way") she lessens the possibility of embarrassing her classmate. Mothers who compliment their daughters set the tone.

Mothers can also help girls make friends by providing a home that welcomes teenagers, a home with a "lived-in" look. Adolescents know when they are wanted; when a house is comfortable, girls are more apt to bring friends around. For many girls, their bedrooms are the entertainment centers and they can spend hours with good friends, closed off from the rest of the family. If it is a coed group, insisting on an open-door policy is wise and sensible parenting. Also, mothers need to develop a tolerance for music they may not like and make sure their kitchens can be invaded by hungry teenagers.

Keeping friends

The anger in girls who think their friends have betrayed them, turned against them, or are plotting to do something without them borders on rage.

Conflict between friends can occupy a major portion of a girl's early adolescence. While most girls solve their own arguments, forget about them quickly, and don't need to talk about them, other girls seem to be constantly feuding and changing friends.

If conflicts erupt often, there may be underlying problems. James Youniss and Jacqueline Smollar from the Center for Study of Youth Development interviewed over one thousand adolescents between ages twelve and nineteen and identified some problems girls and boys encounter with friends.

The research found that not being trustworthy was the biggest problem in adolescent girls' friendships. A girl who can't keep a secret, talks behind a friend's back, gets others into trouble, lies, and steals friends or breaks promises doesn't keep good friends. [2]

Friends honor trust. It's tempting to gossip about a girl who was liked yesterday but not liked today. However, if a girl realized that talking about someone today could boomerang and hurt her tomorrow, she might be less likely to do it. A mother should tell her daughter that if she is untrustworthy or talks behind her friends' backs, she will have trouble making and keeping friends.

When a girl has a problem with a friend, she should try to resolve it directly with the friend and *not* bring everyone else in the group into the discussion. Those who effectively settled problems with friends, according to the Youniss and Smollar study, talked directly to them or offered and accepted apologies. But 26 percent never resolved their difficulties at all, terminating the friendship. Girls need to know that if they cannot resolve problems with friends they will find themselves isolated.

Teenage girls, not unlike adults, crave respect. When a girl makes fun of others, or is snooty, rude, bossy, or argumentative, she may lose her friends. However, she may not recognize that what she is doing shows a lack of respect.

One mother said of her daughter: "She tends to be bossy, so anxious to please that she doesn't know what she wants and at the same time demands her own way and gets angry. She can be loud, silly, immature, and can say hurtful things."

Most mothers, however, don't understand why their daughters do not make friends easily. They know their daughters would make someone a wonderful friend.

Difficult personalities or unacceptable social traits, in fact a whole group of unpopular behaviors, can cause a teenager to be ostracized, according to the Youniss and Smollar research. Although adolescents usually have a tolerance for unusual behavior, they do not stomach it for long in their close friends.

In the study, teenagers identified the behavior that disturbed them: a girl who talked too much, was too moody, drank too much, had a bad temper, was conceited, lied, was stubborn, was spoiled, bragged, acted stupid, or smoked pot. The girls I talked to didn't want friends who acted like that either. They also warned that girls can change in junior high, so that a friend who their mother thought was so outstanding in fifth grade may be a different person two years later.

Frustrated that her mother was promoting a friendship with someone that she didn't like, one girl said, "She's really changed and my mother still thinks she is the innocent girl she was years ago." This mother would be wise to listen carefully to her daughter's comments. Girls are more in tune with what is happening to their peers than mothers are, and mothers should trust their daughters' judgments.

Accepting her friends

Once a daughter acquires friends, then the issues change. Instead of worrying that she doesn't have friends, the mother worries about her selection of friends.

"The family values of her new friends are different than ours, and I don't want them influencing her," fretted one mother.

"My daughter likes the popular group," added another. "But they don't have similar interests. They're too mature for her."

"Why," chimed in a third mother, "is she attracted to the 'in' crowd? They're the ones that get into trouble."

All of these women have daughters who are attracted to friends who are on the fast track. The ten- to sixteen-year-old, without the benefit of hindsight, can gravitate to a group that thrives on danger, while the older adolescent knows that in the long run certain behavior is destructive, because she has seen friends get into trouble.

I asked many girls what a mother should do if she doesn't like her daughter's friends. The responses varied, but there was a common caution that mothers should not forbid a daughter to see a friend because that makes the situation worse. And at the same time, these girls urged mothers to take a forceful stand if the friend was involved in drugs or with a drug dealer.

"I don't mind if she comments about my friends," said one girl, "as long as she doesn't keep me from being with them. She can say I don't like your going out with him, but not to let him in the house is a different story."

"She shouldn't be negative about it, but she should point out the things she questions about the person. Be honest but positive," suggested a girl who, although she could understand a mother's concern, didn't really know how best to deal with the problem.

It was difficult for most of the girls to put themselves in their mothers' shoes. A teenager has so much vested in friends—an openness, a trust, an acceptance that enriches her life and that she can't replace. When her mother doesn't like her friends, she is hurt.

"My mother doesn't like any of my friends," confided a restless high school junior. "If they call up, she pretends I'm in the shower. My friends know she is lying because sometimes she says I'm doing my homework and they know I'm not doing my homework—ever."

When I asked a girl whose mother did not want her to go out with certain friends how she complied with her mother's wishes, she retorted, "You tell her what she wants to know." Obviously, she was not telling her mother the truth.

Girls want their mothers to like their friends and get upset when mothers try to point out their flaws. One girl whose mother wanted her to "upgrade" her friends said, "My mom will pick out my best friends and say, 'Look at her, she's not going to college. She gets bad grades. What future does she have? So you want to be like them?' I say, 'Those are my best friends, stop it.' "

Girls were incensed if mothers disapproved of friends because of race, ethnic background, or economic level. They resented any interference with friends because of nonbehavioral differences, but they understood their mothers' concern if the friend was a troublemaker.

Girls will assist rather than desert friends in trouble, even if they don't approve of their actions. This type of friendship can unnerve a mother who wonders why her daughter wants to hang around with a boy or girl who is constantly fighting with parents, whose parents are fighting with each other, who spends too much time in school detention, or who seems to have serious drinking or drug problems.

She wants her daughter to associate with the winners, those who don't have major problems, come from strong families, are motivated, participate in school activities, and are good students.

But being good friends means helping friends, especially in adolescence when so many feel misunderstood. A girl who was in an alternative high school told me, "My friends are all I have." She had left her mother's home, was living with a friend, and had little contact with her father. Without friends' support, she would have been on the streets.

What does a mother do when she wants the best for her daughter, understands her desire to help her friends, but in her heart realizes that these friends are not good for her? It is important, but not always easy, to remain positive. "Putting them down" can create bad feelings. A mother must remember that these friends are young, too, and many of them are going through difficult times of their own.

Having said that, I want to stress that a mother's first concern should be her daughter, not her daughter's friends. A girl must be told that she is her mother's primary interest, that her mother loves her and likes seeing her happy. After a mother gets those points across she can then share her concerns about her daughter's friends.

"Tell me about Sandy. I know you like being with her. Can you tell me why?"

"I'd like to know Jackie better; tell me about her."

"Tell me why you like being with Tim. Help me understand why you like him so much."

"You don't seem happy after you've been with Jason. Do you want to talk about it?"

When a girl articulates her feelings about a friend, she may help her mother understand why she likes the person so much. Or she may clarify things for herself and decide that the reasons for the attraction are that he or she is daring, different, "off-the-wall," takes risks, captures attention, or pays attention to her only when he or she wants something from her.

The more she talks about her friend, the more she may realize that it is not a sharing and equal friendship. Perhaps she will understand that by acting as her friend's constant listener, or provider, or fall guy, or therapist, or front, or messenger, she is giving everything—and not benefiting in return.

After listening, a mother should be forthright in expressing her concerns to her daughter. If the friends are part of a drinking crowd, the talk should be about her safety. If the group skips school, the importance of a high school degree when she tries to find a job should be emphasized. Self-examination on a mother's part is critical to understanding what bothers her about her daughter's friends and to being able to articulate her worries.

By emphasizing concern for her daughter and *not* belittling her friends, a mother communicates her love. If her doubts about these friends are based on observing the friends' negative effects on her daughter, not on superficial reasons, concealing those reservations would be dishonest and may bring possible harm to her daughter.

Peer pressure

The teenagers I interviewed argued that friends could not pressure them to do something that they did not want to do. They were quite adamant about this, although some admitted that if a friend was doing something they liked, they would join in. They did not equate joining in with responding to peer pressure. The phrase "peer pressure" was a red flag to them. There was no such thing, they claimed.

As much as I would like to believe their protestations, the girls certainly mirrored the dress, expressions, hair styles, and interests of their friends. The distinction finally dawned on me: it is a matter of definition. "Peers" are the great masses of adolescents; "friends" are girls or boys they like. Girls may not be swayed by "peer" pressure, but "friends" have influence.

One girl who smoked cigarettes conceded, "If you like smoking cigarettes and you're sitting in a room and everyone is smoking, you'll smoke. If you like chocolate cake, and everyone's eating it and you're sitting there with saltines, you'll start eating chocolate cake." But she remained convinced that if her friends were involved in something unacceptable (she could not think of an example), she would not join in.

"I found I've been respected more for the things I don't do," said a high school sophomore who took the opposite tack. "Almost everyone started smoking for the wrong reasons in seventh grade and now they have the habit. I never started smoking and now I'm one of the few in my crowd who doesn't smoke and I think I get respect for it."

Laurence Steinberg of the University of Wisconsin found in his many studies of adolescents that seventh- and eighth-grade girls may be the most vulnerable to peer pressure. However, the girls in his research who described themselves as "self-reliant" showed more individuality and more resistance to their peers and were less susceptible to pressures to conform. [3] The sophomore who resisted smoking when her friends took it up in seventh grade exuded a sense of herself throughout our conversation. I believed her when she said she felt respect from her friends for not going along with the crowd.

Steinberg stressed the crucial role of mother in developing a girl's inner strength ("self-reliance") to resist pressure. By confirming her good decisions and giving her opportunities to participate in family decisions, mothers nurture that inner strength. Peer pressure is a factor in teenagers' lives, no matter how much they dislike the term. However, confident mothers—and good friends—can outweigh a peer-group mentality.

MEMOS FOR MOMS

TO HELP YOUR
DAUGHTER MAKE
FRIENDS

Encourage her to:
1. Join activities that attract the type of person she likes.
2. Find out what others' interests are and ask about them.
3. Go out of her way to say something nice or pay a compliment to a classmate.
4. Refuse to talk behind another girl's back.
5. Show the other person she can be trustworthy.
6. Apologize if she hurts another and accept apologies if she has been hurt.
7. Pay attention to her new friend, call, and include her in activities.
8. Be the kind of friend to others that she would like to have.

WHAT MOTHERS CAN DO

1. Share your awareness that making friends is not always easy.
2. Supply companionship during difficult times.
3. Make sure your home welcomes teenage exuberance.
4. Develop a tolerance for loud music, active kitchens, and bedrooms used as family rooms (with an open-door policy for coed groups).
5. Be generous with your share of driving, chaperoning, supplying food for school functions, and participating in her activities.

TO UNDERSTAND HER CHOICE OF FRIENDS

1. Recall how important friends were to you as a teenager.
2. Try to appreciate the qualities she likes in her friends.
3. Emphasize the positive when discussing her friends.
4. Understand her need to spend more time with friends.
5. Acknowledge friends' needs to share and needs for privacy.
6. Appreciate her friends' support of one another.
7. Never criticize a friend because of race, ethnic background, or economic status.
8. Emphasize your concerns about her instead of putting down the friend, if you find valid reasons not to like her friends.
9. Do not tolerate friendships that are destructive to her, again stressing your concern for her, not your dislike of the friend.

9

♥

"But I only had half a beer."

THE ALCOHOL AND DRUG SCENE

♥

Early steps in prevention
Types of alcohol or drug use • Factors influencing use
What to look for in the home
What to notice in her behavior • Memos for moms

❤ The adolescent social scene does not consist of well-chaperoned parties at which soft drinks are served. National surveys estimate that more than 90 percent of high school seniors drink alcohol at some time and up to 50 percent try marijuana. A culture such as ours, which promotes drinking and tolerates marijuana, invites a collision between adolescents who want to experiment and mothers who are concerned about their children's health and safety.

A mother in my workshop told me she was called by the high school principal because her daughter arrived in class reeking of beer. The girl and her friends, unable to resist a beautiful spring day, had gone to the beach with their lunches and a case of beer. Returning to her afternoon classes and unaware of her telltale breath, her daughter asked the teacher a question. After being suspended from classes for a week, the girl was mystified by the furor she caused. "But," she protested, "I only had half a beer."

Experimenting with alcohol may be typical of teenagers, but that does not mean it should be condoned by parents or school authorities. Once upon a time only boys tested the social limits placed on them by their parents and the law.

Now adolescent girls eagerly join the boys in their furtive rounds of unchaperoned parties and underage drinking.

Some girls told me they began sampling alcohol and drugs when they were in sixth grade. "That's the time I got into most trouble," said a junior in high school. "That's the time parents have to decide how they're going to be. They have to let their kids know how they feel about alcohol and drugs." The parties weren't frequent in junior high, another girl said, but they were wild.

These same girls now talk sadly about some of their friends who didn't make it. They were the experimenters who turned into addicts, who "got hooked in junior high." What started out as fun and daring when parents weren't home ended in broken lives for some of their good friends. Most who talk about their experimenting, however, are now well-adjusted seventeen- and eighteen-year-olds who survived their early adolescence. Let us hope their mothers have come through intact as well.

Teenagers need time together. However, when adults are not visible, experimenting with alcohol and drugs can flourish. Being aware of where the local junior and senior high school students are congregating after school and at night is important for mothers. For their daughters' sake, they should become familiar with the local social scene.

Early steps in prevention

A mother faces a multitude of fears about her daughter and alcohol. Will her daughter drink too much and get into an accident that will leave her dead or impaired for life? Will she be drawn into the dark world of addiction and illegal activities, introduced through casual use of marijuana? When her daughter is drinking will she be able to say no to sexual intercourse? Or will she become dependent on alcohol or drugs to weave her way through adolescence?

If a mother dwells on all these dangers awaiting her daughter after (and even sometimes before) her twelfth birthday, she may long for a safe place to sequester her child. However, mothers can rest assured that most girls do *not* get so caught up in this subculture that they fail to emerge into adulthood. Even so, mothers do need to be aware of what is happening, even when a daughter is not involved. It just makes good sense to be aware—the first step to good antidrug parenting during adolescence.

"I know," a girl told me, "that if I go home smelling of beer or pot or incense or liquor or cigarettes, she'll smell it. Wine coolers are harder to detect because they smell like mint, but she knows." This is an aware mother.

Recognizing the allure of underage activities to teenagers is the second step in good antidrug parenting. If a mother does not admit the possibility that her daughter will be attracted to drinking and smoking, then she does not understand or remember what it is like to be an adolescent. Some girls get a thrill from showing their independence by defying the family norm. Others get an added exhilaration from being able to fool a naïve mother. When the dominant activity of a teenage group is getting away with underage drinking or taking illegal substances, then doing these things with friends is very tempting.

Besides becoming aware of the local adolescent scene and the appeal of underage drinking, mothers and fathers have to become conscious of the example they are setting.

"It's a lot to do with role models," advised a high school senior. "When I look at friends' parents who have problems or who don't get along with their kids, I can see why my friend drinks too much. When she comes home after drinking, her dad always has a drink in his hand. It has a lot to do with contradictions. If you see your parents drinking a lot and coming home drunk, you're just conditioned by it."

Another girl told about her parents' gullibility. "We were all in the attic smoking and we were caught," she said. "When my mom and dad came to pick me up they asked me if I had been smoking. I said I had just taken a drag to see what it was like and they believed me. When we got home they hugged me and told me how awful it was for me to have that peer pressure. I was fourteen and already smoking a lot."

This girl later said that her parents still do not know she is smoking even though she has been doing so for three years. I found that hard to believe until she mentioned that her father smokes. The smell of smoke is present in the house, so her cigarette odor is not obvious and her smoking eludes them. His example conceals her behavior.

Drinking is legal for adults, and drinking in moderation does not set a bad example for adolescents. However, any kind of parental participation in illegal drugs tells a girl or boy that fooling the system, avoiding getting caught, and getting stoned are accepted standards of behavior. Even a parental attitude of tolerance of illegal drugs can influence adolescents. When they receive that message or observe those actions in their parents, they don't learn how to put on the brakes to avoid plunging into the world of drugs.

Some children whose parents are not lenient about drugs also descend into the drug world. A reporter wrote in the *Wall Street Journal* about his son's death due to cocaine addiction. His experimenting with marijuana at age twelve led him to the coroner's block at age sixteen. As I read the story, the naïveté of loving parents became apparent. Here were good parents, not aware of the availability of alcohol and drugs in their community. When they first learned of their son's problem, they were relieved to find he was using "only" marijuana, denying the insidious effects of any illegal drug.

If they had participated in school drug-awareness programs,

they might have realized that not only is marijuana itself dangerous for adolescents; it is known as the "gateway" drug, opening the door to harder drugs. They also might have picked up signals from their son's behavior that he was slipping into serious trouble. They didn't know the signs of drug addiction and their child manipulated them—a sad story from caring parents.

If a mother becomes aware of the availability of alcohol and drugs in her community, is conscious of an adolescent's attraction to forbidden pleasures, and is a good role model, will this guarantee her daughter's noninvolvement in these high-risk ventures? Those are good steps to take, but the problem of high-risk behavior is more complex, and factors like a girl's personality, her friends, and her family's style of parenting are important influences.

Also, not all use of alcohol and drugs foretells addiction. A look at different types of usage will help mothers assess their daughters' behavior.

Types of alcohol or drug use

First, I want to distinguish between underage alcohol consumption and illegal drug use. Since alcohol is a legal drug for adults, its use by adolescents is more widespread and often less indicative of self-destructive behavior. The use of illegal drugs, however, beginning with marijuana, signals a more troubling type of adolescent deviance. Although I am not minimizing the seriousness of underage drinking, I am emphasizing that parents should see a red alert if their daughters, or sons, are using marijuana.

Douglas Kimmel and Irving Weiner in their book, *Adolescence: A Developmental Transition*, distinguish four categories of alcohol or drug use by adolescents.[1] For the sake of simplicity, I will refer usually to alcohol, but the same conditions apply to illegal drugs. In the first category of experimental use, an adolescent drinks to see how it tastes or to know why people drink. If, after experimenting, she decides the alcohol scene is not for her and that there are better ways to enjoy herself, she certainly does not have a problem. She is an experimental drinker.

On the next level, a girl drinks socially with her friends, usually in a home when parents are away or at a teenage gathering place beyond adult supervision. If this social setting is the *only* time a girl drinks and she seldom drinks heavily, chances are her behavior will not lead to alcohol dependency. However, she still should know that her mother and father expect her to withstand the social pressures to drink.

The path to dependency for some adolescents originates in experimentation, moves to social drinking, and then escalates to more problematic behavior. I would be especially concerned about marijuana at this social stage because of the added risk of using drugs and the eagerness of drug dealers to keep in business and to push users to the next stage.

The third category of drug use is a medicinal use of alcohol or drugs, described by Kimmel and Weiner as the taking of these substances to relieve anxiety, to feel better, or to enjoy the experience of feeling high. At this level, the adolescent, in order to deliberately induce the euphoric mood, begins to drink or take drugs more frequently, either alone or with selected friends. She may be buying the alcohol or drugs herself rather than waiting until she goes to a party. A family argument or a disappointment with a friend can trigger the excuse for its use, and she begins to depend on the highs to get over an uncomfortable situation. She may move into multidrug use or combine alcohol with marijuana or harder drugs to induce better highs. A girl who has progressed to this third stage needs help to stem her increased dependency on mood-altering substances.

The individual use of alcohol or drugs can lead to the fourth level, that of complete dependency and addiction. The user needs more and more highs to get through the day and dreads being without a supply of liquor or drugs. When the supply is unavailable she will go to extremes to find it, and her physical and psychological resources are absorbed in getting through the lows and to the highs. She has become both physically and mentally dependent on alcohol or drugs to continue her life, and the withdrawals are painful. Her personality changes as her dependency deepens, and she needs professional help immediately.

Factors influencing use

Most adolescents are caught up in the first or second categories of use. The girls either experiment, get sick, and give it up, or they continue to drink with friends at weekend parties. Although a mother should definitely be aware of that behavior and invoke strong consequences when she discovers her daughter is drinking, she should not be too shocked. Her daughter's behavior is adolescent and may not necessarily lead to dependency *if* she has been taught the serious effects of drinking or drug use.

Her personality, her parents' attitudes, and her choice of friends also can be factors in keeping her from slipping into heavier alcohol or drug use.

PERSONALITY

A study conducted by Jack and Jeanne Block of the University of California, Berkeley, and Susan Keyes of the University of California, San Francisco, looked at the personalities of fourteen-year-olds who used marijuana or hard drugs. Girls who used marijuana tended to be rebellious and nonconforming, unable to delay gratification. They valued their independence, but not with the same energy and resourcefulness found in nonusers. Their independence surfaced as hostility, without the nonusers' ambition, self-confidence, or initiative. The harder drug users (using more than marijuana) were seen as even more emotionally bland, distrustful, and self-defensive than marijuana users.[2]

There is a difference between adolescents who seek to be independent and creative as part of the normal process of growing up and those who turn to destructive behavior to display their differences. A "constructively deviant" adolescent, a term used by researcher Laurie Chassin and her colleagues from Arizona State University to describe teenagers who probably are not headed for serious problems, may be curious or adventurous, even experimenting at times, but she is unlikely to self-destruct. She values academic success too highly to threaten it, and while she questions and sometimes rejects her mother's ideas, she is not defiantly rebellious.[3] Her parents have high expectations for her and are responsive to her needs.

"You have to judge your own kids," said a high school senior who could be called a "constructively deviant" teenager. "My mom talks to me a lot. I experimented, but now I don't drink. I don't do drugs. Occasionally I have a few beers, but I would never drive drunk because of their trust in me. I try to live up to their expectations."

Adolescents may experiment, but their personalities and ambitions can protect them. And even if they are rebellious and hostile, their family or friends can help divert them from alcohol or drug dependency.

FAMILY

I talked earlier about an adolescent girl's heightened consciousness of her mother's personality, attitudes, and values. Although she may protest her mother's standards, she is incorporating them into her own developing ideas of appropriate behavior as she begins to differentiate between the standards of her family and those of her friends' families.

Teenage girls are especially influenced by their families' parenting, according to researchers Block, Block, and Keyes. Mothers agree with this finding, remembering the influence their mothers had on them in their own adolescence.

An indifferent or unorganized family does not provide an adequate behavioral structure for a girl because she cannot figure out her family's expectations. This laissez-faire attitude implies acceptance of anything the girl chooses to do, including using marijuana or getting drunk. In addition, parents who themselves abuse alcohol or use and tolerate marijuana are providing dangerous role models for their children.

Mothers who are direct in communicating their values and expectations for their daughters are more likely to have daughters who avoid dangerous use of alcohol and any type of drug. Dr. Judith Brook[4] and her colleagues from the Mt. Sinai School of Medicine in New York City found that a teenager who did not receive positive reinforcement from her mother and who had friends who took drugs had more of a chance of becoming involved in serious use of drugs. When the daughters feel a warmth and affection from their mothers, they are more apt to respond to their mothers' expectations.

A responsive mother also understands that adolescents need controls. For instance, she realizes that leaving a home unsupervised may put her daughter into a situation that she cannot control. Having a few friends over can escalate into a party with alcohol and drugs, whether her daughter wants it or not.

Many teenagers enjoy drinking wine during family cele-brations or rituals. This inclusion of young people in special occasions demonstrates an appreciation of their growing up and demonstrates that family and friends can drink moderately while celebrating or socializing. This custom introduces ad-olescents to a normal, pleasant use of alcohol. Adolescents need to see that adults don't have to drink too much to have a good time, and that some adults don't have to drink at all to have a good time.

Some mothers believe, however, that their children should learn how to "drink" within the confines of their home. This not the same as including teenagers in family cele-brations or rituals. Teaching their children how to "drink" may be their choice but when they include other teenagers in this venture it becomes dangerous and violates other fam-ilies' standards. These parents rationalize serving alcohol to their children's friends by saying, "If they're going to drink, I want them to drink here." They think they are reducing the risks by taking away the car keys, so their underage guests will not drive home under the influence of beer. Not only are these families giving a message that they sanction under-age drinking, but in most states they are jeopardizing their own financial security because they are liable for any acci-dents, in or out of their homes, if they have served teenagers a drink.

Some mothers tell their daughters to call them for a ride home if they or their friends have had too much to drink—no questions asked. This is a sensible approach. If a mother receives that telephone call too often, she will know that her daughter or her daughter's friends need help coping with the local social scene.

By understanding the pressure from friends to drink and conveying that understanding to her daughter, by remaining firm in her conviction that junior high and high school chil-dren should not drink, and by demonstrating warmth, support, and love for her child, a mother facilitates her daughter's passage to a healthy adulthood.

FRIENDS

In addition to a girl's personality and her family style, friends play a big role in determining a girl's attitudes toward drugs and alcohol. How can a child survive being brought up in a neighborhood overrun with drugs? we wonder. Any one of these three factors—her disposition, her family's support, or the help of friends—may influence her to take a path different from that of her neighbors.

Adolescent girls do not want their friends to become dependent on alcohol or drugs (unless they themselves are selling drugs). Although we hear about peer-group pressure—and there is a lot of pressure on teenagers to conform to the accepted social scene—adolescents really don't expect or want their drug or alcohol use or their friends' use to go beyond the experimental or social stage.

Girls who get involved in alcohol or drugs in early adolescence are usually trying to fit into the social scene. "Ninth grade was my lying year," admitted a senior in high school. "Drinking starts earlier, but that year you're all psyched up to go to parties and get drunk and parents don't suspect it yet. In ninth grade there is a lot of sneaking around. You can't drive, so you bring bags of liquor."

She later told me to tell parents that *if* they have any suspicions, they should check the bags kids are carrying to parties. A friend added, "Check the bag of clothes if they're going to sleep at a friend's house." Someone is going to supply the alcohol at a party and by checking once in a while, mothers can prevent their daughters from being the supplier.

One mother I know suspected something when she heard her daughter rummaging around in a seldom-used closet.

When she later noticed her daughter carrying a large bag as she was going out, she asked to see what was in the bag. Much to her daughter's discomfort and the mother's dismay, she discovered that her daughter was bringing hard liquor to a party. This fifteen-year-old had taken the liquor from an adult party, where she was helping to waitress, and had concealed it in the house.

Some girls think that by instigating or joining in drinking or drug-taking they will acquire more friends. However, a "friend" who is using a girl as a source of alcohol is not a friend. Mothers can talk with girls about their responsibilities to themselves and their friends as well as the qualities to look for in friends.

A teenager who lacks the inner resilience to withstand the pressures to conform and finds herself immersed in the alcohol or drug world gravitates to those classmates who themselves are dependent on those substances and she gets deeper into trouble. Her friends who are the experimental or social drinkers drop away, and she now spends a lot of her time talking with other heavy users about getting high and trying not to get caught by their parents or the authorities. How can a mother know when her daughter has arrived at that state?

What to look for in the home

A mother may be saving her daughter's life if she picks up signs of drug use early, before her daughter becomes totally dependent on alcohol or drugs.

Drs. Harold Voth and Gabriel Nahas, pioneers working to save children from drugs,[5] and Ken Barun, a recovered addict who was on the National White House Council for a Drug-Free America,[6] urge parents to search a child's room when they suspect any use of drugs. This is not an invasion of a girl's privacy; it is an effort to help a child who is not able to help herself.

Some mothers I've talked to would not hesitate to go in and clean their daughters' rooms, yet they are reluctant to conduct periodic searches for signs of drug paraphernalia or bottles of liquor—even after they've noticed a disturbing change in their daughters. Dr. Voth reminds us that a mother would act immediately and get professional advice if her daughter had a life-threatening disease. Alcohol or drug addiction can be life-threatening and seriously jeopardize a young person's future, so a mother should act immediately if she suspects a problem.

Teenagers can be clever about hiding evidence of drug use. Books on how to hide drugs are sold in "head" shops, and drugs can be concealed behind walls, in garages, or in more obvious places, like under a mattress. Some adolescents, perhaps wanting to be caught, are not as careful about hiding drugs and only partially conceal them in drawers.

There are several ways to detect drug use. The smell of marijuana is sweet and very distinctive. Adolescents—and adults—often camouflage the odor by burning incense or using room deodorants.

Parents need to be more knowledgeable about the dangers of marijuana. Marijuana contains over four hundred different chemicals, some of which are fat-soluble (not like alcohol, which is water-soluble), and it takes about *thirty days* for the effects of *one* joint to leave the body. If a girl is smoking only one joint of marijuana a week, she will *always* be "under the influence," as the chemicals accumulate in her body. Dr. Voth reports that the brain and the reproductive system retain the highest concentration of marijuana chemicals. The potency of the drug now available is five to ten times higher than when some parents smoked it, and adolescents whose bodies are in the second most important stage of growth are taking grave risks with their health, primarily with the development of their brains and reproductive systems.

Parents must be able to recognize all types of drug paraphernalia. Packets of rolling papers, "roach" clips (tweezers or something similar used for clamping the end of a butt to prevent the fingers from being burned), or pipes are used in smoking marijuana. Water pipes, bongs, or other types of pipes may be found if a child is free-basing cocaine or smoking hashish. There will be evidence of syringes if she is injecting drugs, or small spoons and mirrors if she is sniffing cocaine.

Parents need to be conscious of the phone calls she is receiving. Is her group of friends changing? Are calls coming from teenagers who are not like her old friends, and at strange hours? Because drug deals can be conveniently transacted if a girl has her own phone, I recommend having only one telephone line into a house so callers are not isolated from a mother's occasional scrutiny.

Too little or too much money may be a sign of drug use. A girl who is always asking for money with vague excuses to account for the last handout may be buying drugs. Or, if she has money that a mother can't account for, she may be selling drugs. If she has a budget and an allowance, a change in her finances will become evident more quickly. A look at her bankbook once in a while is warranted if a mother is suspicious.

What to notice in her behavior

Most adults know the signs of hangover from alcohol: headache, bloodshot eyes, and vomiting. The signs of drug use are less well known. The symptoms of drug use may sound to some parents like normal adolescent behavior. However, an alert parent will be able to see changes that are not normal in her daughter's personality and behavior and health.

A girl who is more susceptible to colds and always has a runny nose may not have allergies; she may be using cocaine. All drugs will affect overall health as she eats less well or craves sweets.

Her eyes may be bloodshot, so there will be an increased use of eyedrops. The young residents of a youth shelter where I worked were not allowed to wear sunglasses inside. Why? I asked. Drugs make the eyes sensitive to light, I was told; sunglasses make the light more tolerable and cover up drug use. The social workers also needed to be able to look directly into the youths' eyes.

While normal adolescents experience quick mood shifts, upset one minute and acting as though nothing happened the next, the mood of a girl who is taking drugs may change on a long-term basis. She may be down, in a bad mood or depressed, for days at a time. Or, if she is in an excited mood, it seems extreme and not genuine. Does this seem like her normal behavior, or does her personality seem to be changing? A change in her personality and energy level is one of the first symptoms of drug use, and it should not be attributed to adolescence. Most adolescents question their parents, but her confrontations will be more belligerent, unreasonable, with a hostile tone.

A drug user spends more and more time alone, in her room or in the bathroom. She is not grooming herself; she may, in fact, become sloppy in her appearance. Her attention is centering more on doing drugs than looking good.

The change in friends that I mentioned earlier is a significant symptom of increased drug or alcohol use. Adolescents who are using drugs or abusing alcohol are seeking the company of other drug users, forming a network of peers who may not be at all like their earlier friends. If a mother observes this change, she should watch their activities closely and look for other signs in her daughter, like a personality change, a change in appearance, or a lack of interest in school and after-school activities.

One of the most well-documented effects of marijuana is that the adolescent loses her motivation and is unwilling or unable to take measures to reach a desired goal. She wants to do things, but can't figure out how to get from here to there. For instance, she says she wants to go to a college, but she takes courses that don't challenge her, never studies, doesn't join any clubs or activities, and never takes a leadership role in the school. She drifts through her precious adolescent years, waiting for something to lift her into a productive adulthood, and never comes to grips with her own responsibilities. Marijuana use is a sad way to deplete the exuberance and energy of adolescence.

Early detection and immediate help from parents can get a girl back on her normal adolescent path. As one high school senior said, "Parents ask themselves what they did wrong, but if it were a child, not a teenager, they would look at her and say, 'How can I help her?'" Helping a child regain control of her life by seeking professional help or counseling is the most caring move a mother can make.

Most adolescents remain in the social or experimental levels of alcohol or drug use and may not need professional help. If mothers remain open, yet always alert, and offer guidance, affection, and trust to their daughters, their daughters will emerge safely from their experimental years.

MEMOS FOR MOMS

1. Become aware of the adolescent social scene in your community through reading local papers, attending parent meetings, and listening to your daughter.

2. Let your daughter know that you are aware of the availability of alcohol and drugs in the community and that you understand the pressures on her to drink or take drugs, so she can feel free to talk with you about alcohol and drugs.

3. Listen to her concerns about not being accepted if she doesn't drink. If a crowd doesn't accept her because she won't drink, then she is in the wrong crowd. Let her know that.

4. Help her create a few excuses for not participating in a drinking or drug scene. Just saying no is too hard for most adolescents. Ask her what she thinks would be an effective excuse and think of some from your own youth.

5. Do not serve alcohol to her friends. You are breaking the law and are liable in many states for any accident to a minor in your home or on her way home.

6. Let her know that her safety is your primary concern and that you are available to pick her up if she or her friends have had too much to drink.

7. Remember that she is an adolescent and may experiment.

8. Know the signs of alcohol and drug use. Be alert when she comes home from a party.

9. Initiate a trusting relationship and reestablish it after she has broken trust and paid the consequences.

10. Communicate your concerns about alcohol and drugs directly, without sarcasm, threats, or accusations.

11. Assure her of your affection and support. It helps create a family environment that encourages cooperation, not defiance.

10

"Forget it, I don't want to talk about sex."

THE REAL GENERATION GAP

"My mother doesn't know I know."
"You've got to teach them everything." • "That's a cop-out."
"It's no big deal." • "There's a lot of pressure."
"Let them make their own choice."
"It comes back to trust." • Model programs
Memos for moms

❥ "We both looked away from each other while I talked," one mother told me, describing her "sex talk" with her daughter. "It's too personal to talk about," said another, the mother of a thirteen-year-old. These are typical mothers' comments. Even if a mother has been comfortable talking about menstruation, talking about sex with her young adolescent daughter remains awkward. And her daughter doesn't help by turning aside, saying "Forget it."

A mother's hesitation may stem from any number of causes. She could be uncomfortable in revealing her feelings about sexuality. She may think that by talking about sex she is approving her daughter's possible sexual behavior. Perhaps she keeps waiting for an opportune time, but that time never arrives. Her reluctance also may come from hearing conflicting messages from experts who themselves are baffled by the sexual activities of young girls. Or she just may not know how to bring up the subject, relying on the school to do the job. Mothers who read headlines about teenage promiscuity, the alarming spread of AIDS in adolescents, and the high rate of teen pregnancies are justifiably concerned and know they should talk with their daughters.

When these same mothers were young, sexually active (by

"sexually active" I mean having sexual intercourse) girls were considered "bad" girls and hung around the fringes of junior and senior high schools. The new risk-takers, however, may be at the center of school life and seem unafraid of the possible consequences. Fifty percent of the girls in a high school graduating class may have experienced sexual intercourse. Even if a mother focuses on the 50 percent of the girls in the class who remain virgins and don't take sexual risks, she worries about her own daughter.

"My mother doesn't know I know."

The idea that evasion solves the sex question is far from reality. A girl will find out what she wants to know, and her mother should be a source of information. The strongest influence on a young adolescent girl's attitude about sex is her mother, *if* she has a close relationship with her mother and *if* they have talked about sex. A study headed by Kristen A. Moore of Child Trends, Inc., found that daughters whose mothers communicate their own traditional views about sex are less likely to engage in premature intercourse.[1] Other studies have stressed that any increased communication about sex reduces the probability of early sex.

A high school junior told me, "My mother doesn't know that I know about sex." This girl has an aura of sensuality, a deep, earthy voice, and a slightly rebellious look—which would stop most mothers from probing too deeply. When she said her mother was in the dark about what she knows, I could only sympathize with her mother, who probably yearns to tell her daughter that even if she "knows" it all, she doesn't have to "do" it all. But mentioning sex appears too difficult and emotional. That is the dilemma of many women.

Reviews of sex-education programs, presented at a briefing

to the U.S. congressional staff by the Family Impact Seminar, suggest that a combination of parental involvement at school and at home plus emphasis on long-range, "life options" goals for girls work the best in preventing early sexual activity. In evaluating the effectiveness of sex education in the prevention of pregnancy, the report pointed out that although girls acquire valuable knowledge in sex-education classes, attitudes and behavior generally do *not* change.[2]

Sex-education courses, as important as they are, do not replace a girl's mother. A mother is needed to influence attitudes and behavior. And the best time for persuasion is before, not after, a girl is sexually active. If a girl is already active, the discussion may be late, but it is absolutely necessary.

Throughout this book I have stressed the importance of helping a girl develop a strong sense of self-esteem, self-competence, respect for herself, and a good body image. I believe that having sexual intercourse during junior or senior high school detracts from accomplishing these goals. Adolescents need to delay sexual intercourse until they are wise enough to make good decisions, know the consequences of their actions, and are capable of mature love. At the same time, I also believe that discussion about intercourse should *always* be coupled with discussion about preventing pregnancy.

In my workshops, I urge mothers to examine their own values and decide the sexual values they want to pass on to their daughters. We talk about being honest about our own feelings while being fully aware of the experimental, impulsive nature of adolescence and the societal emphasis on sexual attainment.

Most important, mothers do not want their daughters to be hurt. Therefore, besides communicating their sexual values to children, women are obligated to tell their daughters, and their sons, about preventing pregnancy and disease. This is not a double message. It is realistic to stress delaying intercourse until they are able to form a truly loving and long-term relationship. But those teenagers who choose otherwise *must* protect themselves from pregnancy and from sexually transmitted diseases. Girls should know that the only absolutely foolproof method to prevent pregnancy and disease is abstinence. However, they should also know about every other prevention method. It is up to mothers, reaching into their own experience, or talking with their doctor, or reading literature easily obtained from family-planning clinics, to communicate knowledge about pregnancy prevention to their daughters.

"You've got to teach them everything."

With a few exceptions, the girls I interviewed did not *want* to talk with their mothers about sex. As one girl said when I asked, "Yeah, it's right up there with cleaning my room." Another said, "I can't imagine talking to my mother about sex. Maybe if I was raped." Yet each of these young women emphasized that mothers *should* teach their daughters. "Mothers have got to teach them everything, all about social diseases and pregnancy as well as the emotional side," said one.

Not only do the girls share their mothers' ambivalence about discussing sex; they think their mothers are out of touch with the contemporary world. They don't want to disillusion them with the reality of their sexuality.

"I remember when we were in seventh grade," a girl said, laughing. "My mom saw some kids holding hands and she said, 'Aren't they a little young for that?' " Mothers forget that by seventh grade some girls are almost through puberty. Holding hands is an innocent and appropriate way of communicating affection at that age.

Another girl touched on the truth when she said, "In junior high your parents don't want to know you're thinking about sex. They don't want to believe that their little girls are actually thinking about sex in that way."

Holding hands can progress to hugging and kissing and is still suitable sexual behavior between adolescents. The shifts, however, from kissing to petting, from light to heavy petting, and from petting to intercourse are, according to Dr. Greer Fox and Christine Medlin from the University of Tennessee, more serious developmental steps and may indicate a willingness to become sexually "experienced."[3] Adolescents often do not understand that they *can* control their sexual arousal and stop the momentum that was launched by petting. Quitting may be frustrating for the boy or girl, but it *will not* harm either one. They need to be told they can hug and kiss or even pet without going "all the way."

Because accepting their daughters' sexuality may be difficult for some mothers, they are not aware of their daughters' sexual behavior. The same study by Greer Fox, the leading researcher on parental communication about sex, found that mothers often initiate discussions about intercourse and pregnancy prevention after their daughters are sexually experimenting.

Dr. Fox and her colleague Christine Medlin found that mothers who were accurate in their perceptions of their daughters' level of sexual behavior (from holding hands to intercourse) had daughters who reported feeling close and comfortable with their mothers and were satisfied with their relationship with their mothers.

The same daughters were likely to be direct in asking their mothers for sexual information and viewed their mothers as "viable, approachable" sources of information. However, in spite of their mothers' openness, the majority of girls still thought their mothers wanted to know too much.

Both mother and daughter recognize the need for communicating values, feelings, and facts about sex, but *how* to communicate them is seen from each one's perspective. To talk successfully and openly to the satisfaction of both mother and daughter is the challenge.

"That's a cop-out."

Most mothers do not want their daughters to be sexually active during their junior and senior high school years, and the daughters sense this. So when a mother tells her daughter to feel free to talk with her about sex, some girls think this approach is two-faced.

An outspoken girl told me, "You know you're not going to your mom and ask her questions. I don't know why they say that. That's a cop-out."

"She tells me all the time," another girl said, " 'If you ever want to do this, just come to me, no problems, no questions.' But if I came to her and asked her, she'd be in shock. I would feel really uncomfortable coming right out and asking her about sex."

"My mother wants to say I can talk to her and that if I'm going to have sex she wants me to be protected," said a third. "She says it to be a good parent, but she doesn't want to hear it."

Although the girls consider these situations contradictory, they understand that their mothers are trying to be good parents. One girl said, "When you think about it, I'd be scared to death if I knew my daughter was sleeping with someone. If she didn't have a specific boyfriend, that would scare me more. I would try to do something about it. I would let her know I didn't like it."

Mothers have to initiate the discussions about sex in subtle ways since girls don't like being asked directly about sexual involvement. Ideally, an opportunity to talk would automatically present itself. In reality, mothers have to plan the "spontaneous" event. One girl told of being cornered by her mother as she was getting out of the shower—the girl had no choice but to listen. However, one-way listening is a lecture, not good communication.

Television shows or news events have prompted many discussions about sexual relationships. If a mother tries to connect national events to happenings in local communities, headline stories can provide excellent opportunities to get a discussion going. Many teenagers watch soap operas that present hundreds of situations that can initiate discussions about sexual behavior. Often girls will talk about their friends' problems, and that is a good time to direct the conversation closer to home. How would she feel if that happened to her, or what does she think her friend should do? By showing genuine concern for her friend, a mother can demonstrate her caring attitude toward adolescent girls, and her daughter may respond to this sensitivity. A mother can remain firm in her own convictions while expressing understanding of a girl who may be acting differently.

The advice columns in the newspapers also can foster dialogue. Ann Landers often writes about adolescent problems, and a mother can refer to the letters as a starting point. Asking questions, beginning with a "What do you think?" is a better technique for a mother than stating her opinion up front and turning the session into a lecture.

"I think moms should have talks with their daughters about all this stuff in the summer before they go into the seventh grade," said a girl who did not have an opportunity to talk with her mother. "They could go away for a weekend or have dinner together and a mother could tell her daughter that going into seventh grade means things are going to change." A good suggestion.

Other girls thought that seventh grade was too late. They

advised mothers to begin talking "early, early, maybe in fourth grade. A few kids start fooling around at that time." They reasoned that the younger the girl, the easier the conversation, before, as one girl said, "sex was tied in emotionally."

If a mother cannot bring herself to discuss sex openly or listen to her daughter's feelings about sex, then she should counsel her daughter to talk to a doctor, a relative or friend, or a social worker at a family-planning clinic. Although books may answer some questions, direct contact with a trustworthy adult is more satisfactory. That is the purpose of family-planning facilities.

"It's easier to talk to someone who's totally impartial," a girl advised. "It would be so much easier to go to my doctor than to talk to my mother."

"I started having sex when I was sixteen," a girl confided. "My godmother told me she thought I was too young, but she also told me what to do. I wish my mother had told me to protect myself. I could have taken her advice or not, but she should have told me about protection. This could influence your life."

"It's no big deal."

A couple of girls told me that sex is "no big deal" and adults make too much out of it. "It's been overglamorized," said one. "It's the most common thing."

I think her observation represents a growing attitude. Teenage girls have become so familiar with the sex portrayed in the movies, on television (particularly rock videos and the soaps), and in magazines that they don't connect sex and love. Psychologists theorize that an adolescent boy's sexual tendencies are "genital" in nature, while a girl remains more romantic during her adolescent years. However, as girls encounter sex daily through the media, sex becomes "common" and not identified with love, commitment, or romance.

In a Planned Parenthood poll reported by the Children's Defense Fund, 34 percent of the teenage girls polled thought the main reason teens started having sex was because of "peer pressure." Another 17 percent said "pressure from boys" was the reason, 14 percent said "everyone was doing it," another 14 percent said it was out of "curiosity," and 5 percent said "sexual gratification." A scant 11 percent thought a teenage girl had sex because she was "in love with her partner."[4] Sex and love are becoming disassociated in the adolescent mind.

When a mother told her thirteen-year-old daughter about the first news reports of the nuclear accident at the Chernobyl power plant in the Soviet Union, her daughter reacted to the possibility of global extinction by saying, "Oh, my God, I'm going to die a virgin!" A generation ago, she would have said, "I'm going to die before I fall in love!" The significance of sexual intercourse has changed in our society, and mothers who are faced with this attitude have to examine what this means to their daughters.

A senior in high school told me that she first had sex in tenth grade, but now "I'm off it because sex is boring. I don't do sex anymore. I'm not embarrassed about *not* doing it now. I'll come out and say it straightforwardly." In a survey of sexually active Baltimore teenagers, 86 percent of the girls and 81 percent of the boys said the ideal age for first intercourse was older than they had been, implying that they regretted their early sexual experiences.[5]

Can mothers counteract the attitude that sex between unattached persons is the norm? Or that intercourse due to peer pressures or pressure from boys is the norm? They have to try by continually emphasizing the connection of sex to love and commitment. If a mother knows her daughter is sexually active, she must confront the possibility that her daughter will become "bored" and disillusioned with sex. An adolescent does not realize that truly satisfying lovemaking for a woman involves more than "making out." If a mother can talk to her daughter about what real love is, she can help her realize that good lovemaking involves a male who not only loves her but thinks of her feelings and needs while having sex.

If mothers think sex is special, a powerful force that should be reserved for marriage, she should share those feelings. But she should not give the girl the impression that sex is sinful. She has to stress that sexual feelings, longings, and passions are good and natural.

If a mother is comfortable talking about masturbation, then she can assure her daughter that many adolescents masturbate and that masturbation is a natural and safe release of sexual energies. Masturbation will not have any long-term negative effects, as was preached years ago. Many women themselves do not appreciate the clitoris, which is the most highly sexually sensitive part of a woman's body, more sensitive than the vagina. Perhaps mothers themselves, through books on sexuality, should investigate the clitoris, a seldom-discussed but essential part of a woman's sexual functioning.

Imparting these deep emotions to a daughter may be difficult, but a girl appreciates her mother's sincerity and efforts to help her formulate her own feelings. Again, I repeat that a mother's discussions must include pregnancy-prevention information. Even if a mother does not believe in any kind of preventative methods for herself, her daughter will hear about different methods and a mother would be wise to supplement that knowledge.

Parents who don't hesitate to talk about the necessity for alcohol- or drug-abuse prevention should understand that pregnancy or venereal disease can also have devastating effects on an adolescent. It is the mother, as well as the daughter, who is taking a risk by not discussing how to avoid pregnancy and sexually transmitted diseases.

"There's a lot of pressure."

Teenagers pick up the expectations of our society, and to be both sexy and available is a pervasive expectation. When this message is conveyed directly or subtly by her peers or her boyfriend, she may think she has to cooperate to be accepted.

"It gets back to peer pressure," said one girl. "Some kids feel a lot of pressure about sex, and those are the ones who do something before they are emotionally ready."

When a sizable number of teenagers say that peer or partner pressure was the reason they engaged in sex, as the Planned Parenthood poll revealed, then mothers have to face that fact. Keeping in mind that studies by Dr. Greer Fox and others show that a close mother-and-daughter relationship aids in delaying sexual activity, girls who are sexually active may have been pushed over the edge by peers or partners, regardless of their mothers' closeness.

Girls need to know that they will face this pressure. They also need to know that drinking or taking drugs is closely associated with early sexual activity. If a girl has been drinking, she is more likely to succumb to pressure than if she has not been drinking. As one girl voiced her experience, "You don't have sex unless you're drinking."

A review of the research of adolescent sexuality by the National Research Council's Panel on Adolescent Pregnancy and Childbearing found that early sexual activity is "interrelated with other aspects of adolescent behavior, especially risk-taking behavior such as alcohol and drug abuse."

The same report found that a teenager's sexual behavior is influenced by the values, attitudes, behavior, and actions of important people in her young life. Not only do parents have a strong influence, but a girl's friends, teachers, and community leaders affect her sexual behavior. The sexual mores of the community deliver a strong message.[6]

However, the most effective protection against peer or partner pressure of any kind is a girl's feeling of self-reliance, which comes from a trusting relationship with her mother. Adolescents with strong maternal bonds have been found to have positive self-images that are relatively resilient to influence by peers.

A study by Brent Miller and associates from Utah State University also found that teenagers with *moderate and reasonable* levels of supervision and control had the lowest rates of sexual involvement.[7] In other words, very tight control and very lax control were not successful in delaying sexual involvement. When a mother shows confidence in her teenager by establishing reasonable supervision and control, she builds her daughter's ability to make good sexual decisions and withstand pressure.

Self-confidence also comes from knowing what to expect. If a girl realizes that she may encounter insistence, maybe even coercion, to have intercourse, she will be less influenced by flattering overtures and more prepared to resist. At the very least she should be prepared for the reality of peer pressure. Mothers may want to role-play some risky situations with her.

"Let them make their own choice."

"It's the mother's job to stop you from having sex," said a girl who was sexually active at age fourteen and is now, at sixteen, a mother. "It's the mothers' job to inform their girls, to tell them the consequences and to let them make their own choice." I was struck by the very adolescent nature of her remarks. This young girl wanted her mother both to stop her and to let her go. Now that she has lost control of her young life, she regrets her losses and blames her mother, even though she admits she made her own choice.

Girls do have to make their own sexual decisions. The days of chaperoning are over. When I asked what mothers could say to daughters about delaying sexual intercourse, I received many responses and some good advice.

I was surprised at the insistence of the teenagers that mothers should share their knowledge and feelings about sex, because so many girls admitted that they hated talking about sex with their mothers. If a daughter says she has heard it all, one girl advised the mother to say, "But you haven't heard it from me."

Some girls in a group of high school juniors and seniors (some sexually active and some not) spoke so clearly and openly with advice to mothers that their direct quotes bear repeating.

"Let girls feel they don't have to give in to any kind of peer pressure. Try to have them understand that sex should be reserved."

"It should not be given to someone who's going to leave you if you get into trouble."

"Let them know right now that any girl who loses her virginity in junior or senior high does it because she wants to be cool."

"Let them know they're cool if they don't do it."

"Tell them they're going to regret it."

"A girl thinks because everyone's doing it, it must be good and she doesn't understand the consequences of how you're going to feel afterwards or later in life."

"Let them know if they go out and do it, they're just going to regret it. It's something you're never, never going to forget."

I sensed disillusionment in the voices of these girls and wondered if their tough advice stemmed primarily from not being loved by their sexual partners. They had succumbed to sexual pressures before they were ready, and now they wanted other girls to avoid similar feelings of disappointment or abandonment.

A number of girls who were not sexually active said the most important message they had received from their mothers was respect for their bodies. Their mothers told them that their bodies were theirs, and they did not have to give in to any pressure. This advice reinforces a girl's ability to control risky situations, especially if she is under pressure from a boy who may think he is entitled to a sexual conquest as part of his rite of passage to manhood, or who thinks that because he loves a girl he is entitled to have sex with her.

The new phenomenon of "date rape" has been extensively covered by newspapers and magazines. Girls should be warned that sex forced upon them at any time is rape. Even if a girl knows the boy well and likes him, he cannot compel her to have sex. Telling him directly "This is rape and I am going to report you" is one of many suggestions on how to handle the situation. It is not easy, and mothers and daughters would be wise to read up on how to defend against date rape.

A girl may be unwilling to tell a boy no because she doesn't want to lose his affection, so she has to know how to impress upon him that she can like him, maybe even love him, without having sex with him. Having sex does not prove love. There are many ways to show affection, and boys respond to attention, especially if they know a girl is setting limits in their relationship. Sharing activities, feelings, and ideas along with hugging and kissing creates a strong affectionate bond.

Also, sex is not a way to say thank you for a good time. If a girl worries that a boy might expect a sexual thank-you, then she should pay for her half of the dinner or movie.

"It comes back to trust."

Although a mother may get discouraged about her teenager's sexual activities, she should remember that, even if her daughter is not mature enough to make a good choice, it is ultimately the daughter's decision, not hers, to become sexually active. If a mother has talked openly with her daughter and listened to her, encouraged responsible behavior, communicated frequently her sexual and family values, showed strong interest in her daughter's physical and emotional well-being, urged her to respect her body, informed her of the necessity of preventing pregnancy and disease, and affectionately loved her daughter, that is all she can do. "It comes back to trust," one girl said.

In a final report to the U.S. Department of Health and Human Services, Office of Adolescent Pregnancy Programs, entitled *Intrafamilial Sexual Socialization: Patterns and Outcomes*, Dr. Greer Fox reported, "Impact on those children who did receive sex education from their parents was often marked. Communication, however minimal or even inaccurate, may forestall or postpone a child's sexual activity. Further, among those daughters who were sexually active, parental communication appeared related to more effective contraceptive practices."[8]

Teenagers generally think their parents are much more conservative in their outlook than they actually are, and parents often assume their teenagers are more reckless and irresponsible than they actually are. If both a teenage girl and her mother try to be honest and open with each other, communication will improve and the chances of poor decisions and anguish will lessen.

Single mothers who have an active social life are in a difficult position. Their daughters cannot yet distinguish adult behavior from adolescent behavior and can get confusing messages. A mother should be conscious that she may, inadvertently, be teaching her daughter a more casual attitude toward sexual intercourse than she herself thinks is appropriate for an adolescent. Also, a girl values the privacy of her home, and mothers should be aware that bringing male friends into this intimate setting may disturb her daughter's feelings about the security of her family.

Model programs

Although evaluations of sex-education programs are in the developing stage, good results are emerging from one fairly new program. Project Sex Respect (PO Box 97, Golf, IL 60029) is being tested with seventh- to ninth-grade students in twenty-six public schools in the Midwest. The curriculum was developed to promote abstinence among teenagers and includes homework assignments to be carried out by parents and children. The initial evaluations show a marked change in attitude about the merits of premarital sexual abstinence. After participating in the program, the majority of the adolescents endorsed the idea of abstinence.

Mother-Daughter Choices (Advocacy Press, Box 236, Santa Barbara, CA 93102) is an effective discussion, goal-oriented program that originated at the Girls Club in Santa Barbara and is now used throughout the country. Choices brings mothers and sixth-grade daughters together for six weekly two-hour meetings. These sessions are often sponsored by the PTA but may be organized by the mothers themselves. They encourage communication between mothers and daughters in helping daughters set goals for the future. The girls learn skills of problem-solving, decision-making, and goal-setting. They develop confidence in using their mothers as a resource and acquire the inner strength needed to make good decisions in their lives, including sexual decisions. The program is based on strong research that indicates that girls with plans for the future are less likely to take costly risks.

MEMOS FOR MOMS

1. Examine your own sexual values and personal feelings about sexuality.

2. Communicate your sexual values and family values to your daughter. Create opportunities to talk with her often, alone and without interruptions, well before she enters junior high school. Listen to her concerns about boys, dating, sex.

3. Keep trying to open up sexual discussions with her, even if she says she doesn't want to talk about sex. Use television, newspaper articles, movies, or stories about friends to open up discussion. Ask her, "What do you think?"

4. Don't assume she has heard everything from her sex-education classes. She needs to hear it from you. She needs to know that sexual feelings are good and normal.

5. When talking about sexual intercourse, always discuss ways to prevent pregnancy and sexually transmitted disease, both through abstinence (the best way for adolescents) and through prevention methods. This is not a double message.

6. Emphasize the connection between sex and love to help her withstand pressure to have sex just to experience it. Listen to her needs for friendships while letting her know that having sex does not guarantee popularity.

7. Show your appreciation of her sexuality by helping her feel good about her developing body.
8. Be sympathetic to the dilemmas of teenage girls. Don't condemn. Remain understanding of others yet confident of your own values.
9. Become involved with community efforts to encourage the development of communication skills between parents and children.
10. Show your daughter through your own relationship what love, loyalty, and commitment mean.

11

♥

"I like to talk with my mother."

A NEW APPRECIATION OF EACH OTHER

♥

Moving out of early adolescence
Easing the transition: mothers' voices
Take advantage of the moment • Memos for moms

❣ "Our relationship has changed," said a senior in high school. "My mother and I are closer now and I'm able to tell her what goes on. We used to get into a lot of fights, but now I like to sit down and talk with her."

How had they arrived at this point? "Knowing that my mother trusts me," she said, "knowing that she lets me go and kind of fish my way out, makes me like to talk to her more."

Another girl who spoke admiringly of her mother told of a crisis between them that occurred when she was in eighth grade. She had become so drunk she had to be taken to the emergency room of the hospital. Her classmates witnessed the scene, their parents quickly found out, and even the local newspaper ran the story. Her mother was "devastated." Yet they learned to enjoy each other once again.

To discover how they had reached this new level of communication, I asked these two girls if I could talk to their mothers. Those interviews, and others with mothers who were also praised by their daughters, bolstered my belief that a mother and her older adolescent daughter *can* reach new levels.

Whether or not mothers and daughters are satisfied with this new relationship depends on how each one has made the transition from the first signs of a daughter's puberty and her consequent protests to the gradual acknowledgment of their mutuality as women. That recognition of shared gender, expressed uniquely by each woman, makes honest discussion possible in middle and late adolescence.

Moving out of early adolescence

The first shift in a girl's attitude toward her mother comes when she reaches a "rapproachment" phase of their relationship. The term *rapproachment* was first used by psychologists to describe the actions of the two-year-old running back to her mother for reassurance after boldly exploring her surroundings. It was applied to adolescence by Ruthellen Josselson of Towson State University, who observed that teenagers, after asserting their need for independence, want to reestablish peace with their parents. The terms of the peace, however, will not be on the same childlike terms of preadolescence.[1] I think this overture toward harmony can be picked up by an alert mother toward the end of her daughter's high school years.

The attempt to reconcile comes when a girl learns that passive resistance to her mother's encroachment on her independence may be more effective than loud protestations. As she protests less and instead closes her mother out by not responding, the arguments subside. A daughter then has some space and stillness in which to find her own voice, her own expression of ideas and feelings, a voice that does not speak out only in reaction to her mother.

"I think you have to say what you feel and let them know

what your expectations are," said an alert mother, "*but* there are times when they really need to be by themselves. My daughter spent endless hours in her room, not communicating. She needed that."

When a girl discovers her own voice, she realizes that even passive resistance is unnecessary. She no longer worries about being too much like her mother or about having to say what her mother wants to hear. She can honestly and openly disagree.

As she develops more confidence in herself, the young woman can turn to her mother for support and conversation. They can listen to each other and share mutual interests, because the daughter now knows that every conversation does not have to be a one-way lecture.

Not every mother and daughter achieve this mutuality by the end of high school. Sadly, some never attain that level of friendship. Sometimes a mother continues to control or give unwanted advice long after her daughter has attained maturity, and her daughter continues to discount her mother. They must wait longer to achieve mutual understanding.

Easing the transition: mothers' voices

The mothers I interviewed for this chapter were amused at being singled out by their daughters. All realists, they know that there is no such thing as a perfect mother, nor would they particularly want the title. However, it was clear that these women work at trying to understand their teenage daughters and were pleased to be asked about their experiences in guiding them through early adolescence.

MOVING TOWARD MUTUALITY

"Lots of things were negative when she was in junior high," said one mother. "I think kids at that age, no matter what, don't feel good about themselves and so everything you say negative to them makes things that much worse."

To be able to refrain from saying anything "negative" during early adolescence is a remarkable accomplishment. I'm sure there were times when this mother bit her tongue to keep from lashing out in response to an unkind remark from her daughter. Her restraint, however, proved to be productive, since her daughter told me that now she can discuss almost anything with her mother.

After suffering through the "seventh-grade uglies," a mother's apt description of that year I mentioned earlier, a girl will graduate to what another mother humorously called the "eighth-grade mouth." She said that while she didn't like her daughter "mouthing off" when she was in junior high and insisted on respect, she didn't take the comments personally. She knew that it was typical of most eighth-graders and that her daughter would eventually outgrow the need to talk back.

What these mothers never seem to forget is that they are adults, the guides for the young, and their daughters are children learning to express their uniqueness. The mothers' skill in guiding their daughters comes from not only a respect for their daughters' individuality but also a respect for themselves as mothers.

LIKING HER OWN ROLE

If a woman enjoys her role as a mother of a teenage girl and appreciates the youthfulness of her daughter, the step from helping her during adolescence to mutual cooperation in adulthood will be easier. The women I talked to liked being mothers. Whether or not they worked outside the home had nothing to do with that feeling of affectionate commitment to their daughters.

Role satisfaction has a lot to do with anyone's happiness, and these women were no exception. Yes, they had periods of doubting the value of what they were doing, but those moments passed without crisis. They were able to emphasize the positive aspects of their lives and their daughters' lives.

Their daughters' admiration was partly based on the conviction that their mothers would not abandon them. These girls were not burdens to their mothers; they were not the "throwaway children" of our society. They felt secure in their mothers' affection.

BEING THERE

A number of mothers told me that availability was key to getting to know their daughters during early adolescence, a key that brought them and their daughters to an appreciation of each other in late adolescence. When they talked about availability, they did not mean they stayed home all the time but that their daughters knew they were "there" for them.

I asked a mother who worked full-time how she happened to understand teenage girls so well. Surprised at my question, she responded, "By just being there when they need me."

She said that her children know they can telephone her at her office at any time. They always get through and her associates know who they are. Her children don't hesitate to call because they know she welcomes their calls. She works in the same city where they live, so if her daughter needs anything, she can stop by and "hit me up for it."

"At home when she wants to talk," this mother said, "I stop what I'm doing, *sit down*, and listen. If she's busy and everything is fine, she'll just go about her business and talk to her friends, but if something is eating her, I know." She makes a point of putting down her book or newspaper to "look" available when her daughter walks in the room.

A mother who did not work outside her home explained availability a little differently. "I think what mothering means to me is to *know* your child," she said. "That requires *presence*. Presence is more than being physically present. When you are with them, you are mentally there. I give them the same courtesy we adults provide one another. They deserve that, too. At every stage they deserve that. That's what I try to do and find examples and ways of teaching them without imposing on them."

A mother I know who works in real estate told me she has a car telephone in order to keep in touch with her children. Her daughter knows she can always reach her.

Another mother who had supported her children alone through their earlier years chose to remain home when she remarried, convinced that being physically available during early adolescence was crucially important. She told me about serious trouble among a number of her daughter's friends whose mothers are seldom accessible. "I think," she said, "that young adolescent girls need their mothers, maybe more than any other time."

LIKING ADOLESCENTS

When I walked into the home of one of the successful mothers, I knew in a minute why the girl and her friends had talked so warmly about this woman. She was open and friendly, immediately put me at ease, and talked affectionately about her daughter and her friends.

"If my daughter and her friends are out and don't like what they're doing, they'll come home," she said. "Or, if they want to get away from something, they'll come here and they know

I'm not going to interrogate them. They'll show up at eleven-thirty at night with a group of kids and, as long as they don't tear up the place, they're welcome to use it."

She tries to like all her daughter's friends. Her daughter told me, "My mother would never say anything bad while I was hanging around with someone she didn't particularly like, but after we stopped being friends, she would say something. She waited until I picked up what was wrong."

Her friends say that this mother does not intrude on them when they are at her house, but they frequently choose to seek her out. Several of them told me they felt very comfortable confiding in her or just chatting with her. When I asked the girl if she minded others talking freely to her mother, she laughed and said, "No, she's not pushy. Even I can tell her a lot more than most of my friends can tell their mothers."

If her mother happens to ask one of her friends too many questions, her daughter feels free to say, "What is this, 'Twenty Questions'?" Even though freedom of expression prevails in her home, this mother sets clear limits on her daughter's hours, expects her daughter to work well at school, to have a job in the summer, and to be responsible for herself.

Not every mother possesses an open personality like this woman, but every woman can acknowledge her daughter's friends and be friendly. And adolescents respond to mothers who like them.

"I'm much more relaxed with her because she's my youngest," said another woman, an experienced mother of two older children. "I have time for her to be a teenager."

I think her comment is important. Teenagers need time to be adolescents, especially in this era of high pressure to succeed and high pressure to experiment. They need time to get through their junior and senior high school predicaments. And when an incident becomes a crisis, patience is required.

"One time," said this mother of three, "the floodgates opened up when her stepfather criticized a rough draft of a school paper. She shut herself in her room and would not let me in for ten minutes. Then we talked. She really just needed to cry and express herself. It wasn't just that one thing that was bothering her. Oftentimes this is the case. Things accumulate when you're a teenager."

In contrast, during a workshop, a mother, frustrated by the mood swings of her daughter, said with real pain that she didn't know if she even liked her daughter anymore. I can sympathize with this mother's attitude, but I was concerned about her daughter picking up that message, just when she needs reassurance that she is okay. It is hard to conceal dislike—especially in a family.

I'm convinced that learning about adolescent development makes it easier to like the early adolescent. The more a mother knows about this particular stage of her child's development, the better she will communicate with her daughter. She will not be surprised by her daughter's mood shifts, and she will hear more clearly her child's underlying concerns and fears.

By the end of the four-session workshop, this mother who was struggling to like her daughter was more relaxed, acknowledging that many of her concerns were about normal development. She was delighted to know that her daughter's particularly exasperating behavior would pass with time and patience.

LOOKING BACK OVER A CRISIS

Jeanne Brooks-Gunn and Marta Zahaykevich interviewed pairs of mothers and early-adolescent daughters for a research project on early adolescence. They found, among more than one hundred pairs, only one that said they never had a disagreement.[2]

The well-liked mothers I interviewed confirmed this observation and readily admitted that they and their daughters disagreed on issues frequently, especially when the girls were in junior high. Although they still can disagree with each other, these mothers listen to their daughters' objections, do *not* hold back their own opinions or values, are open to change and negotiation, and at the same time remain firm when the issues are of importance to their family values.

Another trait became evident as I talked with some of them about their successful experience as mothers of adolescents: their ability to forgive their daughters.

I asked the mother of the girl mentioned earlier who was poisoned with alcohol in eighth grade how she overcame this violation of her trust and forgave her daughter, and heard her side of the story.

"I was so upset for her and felt so bad for her. I was surprised she had done it, that she had no sense. I knew also that this was a horrible way of learning a very, very important lesson. There was a discussion about prosecuting the man who supplied them with liquor. The issues were not small. During a big family conference we found out that a whole group of girls had been drinking gin-and-tonics and that her sister, one grade behind her, had also been drinking with them. It really frightened us. The consequences were the usual grounding, but more than that we spent an enormous amount of time talking about it and trying to come to grips with it. This is what drinking is, I told her. This is drunk. This is what it does to you, and alcohol poisoning is a reality. I was angry and disappointed. It was very clear that she had broken the rules of our family and, more important, had broken a trust. It took all summer, but when she told me that she had learned something, I really trusted her."

By forgiving her daughter and establishing a wiser relationship with her, this mother earned her daughter's gratitude and respect. "I have a wonderful relationship with my mother," her daughter, now a senior in high school, says. "My mother has very high values and she has strength. She is able to communicate them to me, and I've talked to her about all sorts of things that other girls won't talk about with their mothers. Of all the mothers I know, she is the one who is able to understand what is happening today with teenagers."

The ability to forgive is strongly associated with a person's ability to nurture, according to a study by John Buri and his associates at the College of St. Thomas in St. Paul.[3] The mother in the above example nurtured her daughter not by condemning her and her friends for their foolish and dangerous behavior but by helping them to find better ways. She wants her daughter to have the strength that she has, including the strength to move on after making a mistake.

THE RIGHT BALANCE

In addition to the ability to listen and forgive, another common thread wove through the discussions I had with these mothers. They all have high expectations for their daughters, not expectations built on imposing their own dreams on them but expectations for the girls' behavior, both in and out of school. They set down guidelines, including curfews, and expect things like homework and household chores to get done— with flexibility. Extensive research by Diana Baumrind and others is documenting that these mothers are right. Adolescent girls need structure in their homes.[4]

In addition to providing homes with a strong structure so the girls know what is expected of them, these mothers also encourage their daughters to figure out the answers to their own difficulties. This is preparing them for adulthood.

"If my daughter gets into a bad mood and everything gets her down, we usually sit down and talk it out," said one mother. "I don't go rushing in and meddling for her. I make her solve her own problems. If something happens at school, I ask her if she would like me to call the school, but I never have to. She always says that she'll take care of it herself."

This response impressed me because, on the one hand, this woman expressed support for her daughter if she needed it, and, on the other, she expressed confidence in her daughter's ability to solve her own problems.

How did she develop that confidence in her daughter? I asked. "I let her do things on her own, but we also do a lot of things together, as a family. I don't believe in being real strict and I don't believe in being very lenient. I try to be in the middle. Sometimes it's trial-and-error." She made bringing up a teenager sound very easy. No wonder the transition to adulthood was running smoothly for her daughter.

CONFIDENCE IN A DAUGHTER

The other mothers did not make parenting sound easy, but they freely expressed confidence and pride in their daughters. What comes first, I wondered, a mother's belief in her daughter or the daughter's ability to engender confidence and pride? I have always believed that a mother sets the tone by providing opportunities for a girl to feel productive and successful. The mothers I talked with substantiated my conviction.

One, for example, described her daughter's struggle with a learning disability that was discovered in second grade when she could not read or do math. Now a senior in high school, the girl has a strong sense of herself and a confidence in her academic abilities. This self-assuredness did not come easily, but her mother gives her full credit for overcoming her learning handicap. After talking with her mother, however, I would give the mother part of the credit.

When she realized her daughter would need more attention with schoolwork, she did not hesitate to talk with the teachers and to work with her daughter outside of school. She felt it was in the best interest of her daughter to repeat a grade, in spite of the school's recommendation to keep passing her. And she was very sensitive to her daughter's loneliness during those years.

"I felt a special bond with her," her mother says. "I felt a tremendous compassion for her, without wanting to imply that her disability was a negative thing. As a matter of fact it hasn't been negative. It has been very positive for her. It's simply a different way of thinking and approaching her education. The trick is to figure out a way to get this information in.

"I tried to instill in her a sense of her ability and her self-esteem," she continued, "so that no matter what happens, she can deal with it. She has many talents and I knew it. So for a while I was very aware and focused on her. When raising a family, you look to the one who needs you most at a certain time. I knew she needed me."

Another mother talked with pride of her daughter's acceptance of herself, something she herself did not possess in high school. "She's content with herself," she said. "I admire her convictions and her sense of well-being. Mothers want things to be perfect and sometimes put that onto their daughters, but life isn't that way and she knows that. I didn't discover that until I was much older."

Although this mother also would not take any credit for her daughter's good sense of self, her parenting attitudes certainly promoted it. "You have to set guidelines for them, but you have to give them room to grow. They have to learn to make decisions for themselves. Sometimes they may be the wrong decisions, but then they learn, and you hope you can help them learn."

I saw my own daughters grow in confidence whenever they accomplished something on their own. Whether it was a simple project like painting a piece of furniture or a major step like applying for a first summer job, they found out that they could manage, no matter how difficult the task had seemed at first.

Take advantage of the moment.

"When can I expect adolescence to end?" some mothers ask in desperation. Adolescence is drawing to a close when a mother and daughter can sit down and engage in a conversation without admonishments or warnings, without generating guilt on either side, and with genuine sharing. If a mother and daughter cannot reach this point, their relationship may be thwarted, but adolescence still is ending, maybe not satisfactorily, but ending. And a new stage begins in their relationship.

In order to take advantage of the moments that indicate a change in the relationship, mothers must be especially attuned and sensitive when their adolescent daughters are ready to sit down and talk. Opportunities for understanding each other should not be ignored.

When the opportunities are lost, the effect can be shattering. A girl in a homeless shelter described her futile attempts to tell her mother she loved her. She remembered standing at the door of their living room one night, getting up the nerve to go to her mother, kiss her, and tell her she loved her. Noticing her uncharacteristic lingering by the door, her mother had said, "What are you doing? Why are you standing there like that?"

The moment passed, no affection was exchanged, and the girl recalls this episode as a turning point. She turned her back and walked out the door, repressing her tears. She began to skip school shortly after that and started hanging out with the "wrong" people. She could not bring herself again to reenact that moment of exposure, of vulnerability. Would her mother have rejected her embrace? She does not know and may never know.

There are times when a mother must take the first step, sometimes swallowing her pride, and hug her daughter. The occasions may spring up frequently or they may be rare. They may not be noticed, concealed often behind averted eyes, defiant looks, or nasty comments. But a mother can never exclude the possibility that a desire to love her exists within her daughter.

Similarly, a daughter must never abandon the hope that her mother does love her. Even if she thinks her mother's emotional life might be better without her around, or that her mother blames her for a failed marriage, or that her mother disapproves of everything she does or is not interested in her at all, she must at some point approach her mother again. Will she be rejected? She must take that chance.

A friend of mine recently commented that mothers think their attachments to their daughters are so "tenuous" that they are afraid to say anything. They hesitate to be themselves because they think their daughters will reject them. And ironically, I think that is just what daughters want their mothers to reveal—themselves.

MEMOS FOR MOMS

1. Be alert for signs of your daughter's attempts to restore harmony to your relationship. Don't miss the opportunities.
2. Don't let pride come between you. Be open to her.
3. Give her time and space to develop her own voice, her own thoughts, her own feelings.
4. Emphasize the positive about her and about your life with her.

5. Take time to like yourself and enjoy your role as mother.
6. Be there when she needs you, in person or by phone.
7. Allow her time to be a teenager and to be self-absorbed.
8. Become an expert in adolescent development. It makes understanding her easier.
9. Always be willing to forgive, forget, and move on.
10. Provide structure in your home so she knows what is expected of her.
11. Let her solve most of her own problems.
12. Provide opportunities for her to build confidence in her own abilities.

12

And into adulthood

THE MEANING OF THE NEW RELATIONSHIP

Adolescence marks only one of the times in a woman's life when she will redefine her relationship with her mother. If she has not emerged from adolescence with a sense of independence while maintaining a close connection to her mother, does that mean she remains an adolescent? No, adolescence ends when a girl reaches full physical maturity and possesses an *emerging* sense of who she really is.

Adulthood will offer new challenges to a woman, demanding that she constantly rethink what her womanhood means. As she finds new opportunities for growth, she will continue to transform her relationship to her mother. To say, as some experts have, that women remain fixed in a childlike relationship with their mothers or that they transfer their dissatisfaction with their mothers onto their spouses is an affront to the ability of women to reassess their lives at different stages of their development.

Mothers, like daughters, are constantly rethinking their roles and redefining themselves. Often, but not always, they are examining their lives in relation to their children's development, and grappling with the responsibilities they have acquired, usually the care of others. Mothers usually are focused on the "other," whether it is a spouse, a child, or a parent, and they strive to reconcile their concern about others with their rightful concern about themselves and their future.

When I was discussing adolescence with a colleague recently, I was struck by an observation she made. "Because women are so involved with the care of others," she said, "they should be allowed when they are adolescents to be self-centered, to think about themselves first. They may never have that opportunity again."

And that freedom to be self-centered is probably what most mothers fear in their young adolescent daughters. Mothers want them to step into the caring roles they have assumed from their own mothers. When a daughter acts self-absorbed, she is reminded that she must think of others before she thinks of herself. And so she does, into adolescence and adulthood. When a boyfriend belittles her abilities, she accepts his criticism because she wants him to feel good about *himself*. By underplaying her own capabilities, she deprives herself of an essential human need—to feel good about herself.

Then when she thinks about what she really wants, she feels guilty for focusing on herself. The admonitions to care for others are recalled and she is thrown into indecision.

A mother who thinks about her own care and development is not only fulfilling her own needs; she is also providing a strong role model for her daughters—and her sons. By shifting the spotlight from focusing solely on her ability (or inability) to mother and allowing her other talents to be illuminated, she is letting her daughter see her as a real person, not as a mother only. That does *not* mean she gives up her commitment to her daughter or to her family. To the contrary, she enhances her life and their lives.

A mother who was sensitive to the needs of her family, especially her teenage daughters, expressed the anguish of a woman trying to think of herself as a distinct person within her family: "I think my biggest concern as a woman and as a mother of these girls is as a role model in a time of great transition for women," she said. "I think that's been the hardest thing for me, to encourage them to find their own place as young girls and young women, not to be negative about being the mother or homemaker. There are wonderful things that can come out of that."

I asked her to explain why she found it difficult to encourage her daughters. She said, "They have seen the conflict between my husband and me as I have tried to turn away from having only that traditional role. I have not hidden that from them. They see that it causes problems. I have always, rightly or wrongly, allowed them to see my pain in this and sometimes it's very great. And I've tried to talk to them in such a way that they have a positive feeling about me. I say constantly to them that man is not the oppressor and woman is not the victim. A woman chooses, and that choice is painful and hard. My biggest concern is that they will see me as victim."

When I interviewed this woman's daughter, the honesty of her mother's relationship with her was apparent. Her daughter described her mother as strong and caring, a person who has clear values and knows herself. Her mother's struggle with juggling roles in a society that may consider her out of step was looked upon not as a weakness but as a strength by her daughter, who sees and loves her as a real person.

When a young woman in her early twenties heard I was writing a book about mothers and adolescent daughters, she wrote to me about her estrangement from her mother during adolescence. "There was," she wrote, "so much pain, so much anger, so much resentment, so much confusion and frustration, and underneath it all, so much love and need for her acceptance."

At the end of her adolescence, she had sadly concluded, "We could never be friends, only mother and daughter."

Included in her letter was a copy of a paper entitled "Anger," written in college about her relationship with her mother. The process of writing that paper had forced her to confront her repressed feelings, her "nagging pain about a failed relationship with Mom." In a wave of unexpected emotion that consumed her while she was reading her paper out loud in class, she recognized that her mother was too important to cast away without striving to establish even a "fraction" of a relationship. And she made the first move toward reconciliation.

Because her words about their coming together express the yearning of so many daughters to be reunited in a new way with their mothers, I include an excerpt from her letter.

"Perhaps the tensions between a mother and daughter are part of a special rite of passage. Because we—mothers and daughters in general—are so similar we need to assert our independence from one another, or from our roles as mother and daughter, before we can relate on the level of adults. When all of the hostilities between Mom and me were over, we were closer than ever. She was no longer just my mother, that abstraction of an ideal upon which children are dependent, nor was she the flip side of that, an uninterested disciplinarian we confront during adolescence. She was my equal, and she was a friend. I wanted to know about everything she did. For example, I wanted to know all the names of the flowers in her garden—the very garden I had before seen as part of the meaningless life she led. It was important, moreover, that she teach them to me, so we could share what was important in her life. I also began to talk to her about my life and—surprise—she was very interested in and proud of what I had been doing. We were getting to know each other again, opening up, and it felt great."

Every girl yearns to know her mother. This longing may touch a woman at any time in her life. The process of reconciliation begun by many at the end of adolescence may be initiated by either mother or daughter, at any time. It is never too late—because they have not stopped wanting to love each other.

Notes

CHAPTER 1

1. Richard M. Lerner, "A Life-Span Perspective for Early Adolescence," in R. Lerner and T. L. Foch, eds., *Biological-Psychosocial Interactions in Early Adolescence* (Hillsdale, N.J.: Lawrence Erlbaum, 1987).

2. Louise J. Kaplan, *Adolescence: Farewell to Childhood* (New York: Simon and Schuster, 1984), p. 15.

3. Judith G. Smetana, "Concepts of Self and Social Convention: Adolescents' and Parents' Reasoning About Hypothetical and Actual Family Conflicts," in M. R. Gunnar and W. A. Collins, eds., *Development During the Transition to Adolescence* (Hillsdale, N.J.: Lawrence Erlbaum, 1988).

4. Helm Stierlin, *Separating Parents and Adolescents* (New York: Aronson, 1982).

5. Lucy Rose Fischer, *Linked Lives: Adult Daughters and Their Mothers* (New York: Harper & Row, 1986).

CHAPTER 2

1. Jeanne Brooks-Gunn, "Adolescents as Daughters and as Mothers: a Developmental Perspective," in I. Sigel and G. Brody, eds., *Family Research* (Hillsdale, N.J.: Lawrence Erlbaum, 1989).

2. Margaret L. Stubbs, Jill Rierdan, and Elissa Koff, *Becoming a Woman: Considerations in Educating Adolescents About Menstruation*, Wellesley College Center for Research on Women, Working Paper No. 169, 1988.

3. John P. Hill, "Adapting to Menarche: Familial Control and Conflict," in M. R. Gunnar and W. A. Collins, eds., *Development During the Transition to Adolescence* (Hillsdale, N.J.: Lawrence Erlbaum, 1988).

CHAPTER 3

1. Jean Piaget, "The Growth of Logical Thinking from Childhood to Adolescence," in H. E. Gruber and J. J. Voneche, eds., *The Essential Piaget* (New York: Basic Books, 1977).

2. David Elkind, *All Grown Up and No Place to Go* (Reading, Mass.: Addison-Wesley, 1984).

3. Judith Smetana, "Adolescents' and Parents' Conceptions of Parental Authority," *Child Development* 59 (1988).

4. Catherine R. Cooper, "Role of Conflict in Adolescent-Parent Relationships," in Gunnar and Collins, eds., *Development During the Transition to Adolescence* (Hillside, N.J.: Lawrence Erlbaum, 1988).

5. John P. Hill, "Research on Adolescents and Their Families: Past and Prospect," in C. E. Irwin, ed., *Adolescent Social Behavior and Health* (San Francisco: Jossey-Bass, 1987).

6. Carol Gilligan, "Adolescent Development Reconsidered," The Tenth Annual Gisela Konopka Lecture (St. Paul: Center for Youth Development and Research, University of Minnesota, 1987), p. 44.

7. Carol Gilligan, *In a Different Voice* (Cambridge, Mass.: Harvard University Press, 1982). See also Carol Gilligan, Janie Ward, and Jill Taylor, eds., *Mapping the Moral Domain* (Cambridge, Mass.: Harvard University Press, 1988), and Carol Gilligan, Nona Lyons, and Trudy Hanmer, eds., *Making Connections: The Relational Worlds of Adolescent Girls at Emma Willard School* (Cambridge, Mass.: Harvard University Press, 1990).

8. Judith Wallerstein and Sandra Blakeslee, *Second Chances: Men, Women, and Children a Decade After Divorce* (New York: Ticknor and Fields, 1989).

CHAPTER 4

1. Erik Erikson, *Identity: Youth and Crisis* (New York: W. W. Norton, 1968).
2. Julian Rotter, "Interpersonal Trust, Trustworthiness, and Gullibility," *American Psychologist* 35 (1980).

CHAPTER 5

1. Greer Litton Fox, *Intrafamilial Sexual Socialization: Patterns and Outcomes* (Washington, D.C.: U.S. Department of Health and Human Services, Office of Adolescent Pregnancy Programs, 1986).
2. John P. Hill, Grayson N. Holmbeck, Lynn Marlow, Thomas M. Green, and Mary Ellen Lynch, "Menarcheal Status and Parent-Child Relations in Families of Seventh-Grade Girls," *Journal of Youth and Adolescence* 5 (1985).
3. James Youniss and Jacqueline Smollar, *Adolescent Relations with Mothers, Fathers, and Friends* (Chicago: University of Chicago Press, 1985).
4. John Snarey and Anthony Maier, "Fathers' Participation in Childrearing: II. Consequences for Children's Adulthood Outcomes," paper presented at the 96th Annual Convention of the American Psychological Association, Atlanta, 1988.
5. Jeanne Brooks-Gunn, "Pubertal Processes and Girls' Psychological Adaptation," in Richard M. Lerner and Terryl T. Foch, eds., *Biological-Psychosocial Interactions in Early Adolescence* (Hillsdale, N.J.: Lawrence Erlbaum, 1987).

6. Sanford Dornbusch, Ruth Gross, Paula Duncan, and Philip Ritter, "Stanford Studies of Adolescence Using the National Health Examination Survey," in Lerner and Foch, eds., *Biological-Psychosocial Interactions in Early Adolescence.*
7. Judith Wallerstein and Sandra Blakeslee, *Second Chances: Men, Women, and Children a Decade After Divorce* (New York: Ticknor and Fields, 1989).
8. John Snarey and Joseph Pleck, "Fathers' Participation in Childrearing: I. Consequences for Fathers' Midlife Outcomes," paper presented at the 96th Annual Convention of the American Psychological Association, Atlanta, 1988.

CHAPTER 6

1. Earl S. Schaefer, "A Circumplex Model for Maternal Behavior," *Journal of Abnormal and Social Psychology* 59 (1959).
2. Earl S. Schaefer, "Children's Report of Parental Behavior: An Inventory," *Child Development* 36 (1965).
3. Christine Ziegler and Jerome B. Dusek, "Perceptions of Child Rearing and Adolescent Sex Role Development," *Journal of Early Adolescence* 5 (1985).
4. Diana Baumrind, "A Developmental Perspective on Adolescent Risk Taking in Contemporary America," in Charles E. Irwin, Jr., ed., *Adolescent Social Behavior and Health* (San Francisco: Jossey-Bass, 1987).
5. Diana Baumrind, "The Influence of Parenting Style on Adolescent Competence and Problem Behavior," address to the 97th Annual Convention of the American Psychological Association, New Orleans, 1989.
6. Grayson N. Holmbeck and John P. Hill, "Storm and Stress Beliefs About Adolescence: Prevalence of Self-reported Antecedents, and the Effects of an Undergraduate Course," *Journal of Youth and Adolescence* 17 (1988).
7. Sanford Dornbusch, "Individual Moral Choices and Social Evaluations: a Research Odyssey," in *Advances in Group Process*, Vol. 4 (Greenwich, Conn.: JAI Press, 1987).

CHAPTER 7

1. Joan Jacobs Brumberg, *Fasting Girls: The Emergence of Anorexia Nervosa as a Modern Disease* (Cambridge, Mass.: Harvard University Press, 1989).
2. Ilana Attie and Jeanne Brooks-Gunn, "The Development of Eating Problems in Adolescent Girls: A Longitudinal Study," *Developmental Psychology* 25, no. 1 (1989).
3. Joseph P. Allen, Roger R. Weissberg, and Jacquelyn A. Hawkins, "The Relation Between Values and Social Competence in Early Adolescence," *Developmental Psychology* 25, no. 3 (1989).
4. Laurie B. Mintz and Nancy E. Betz, "Prevalence and Correlates of Eating-Disordered Behaviors Among Undergraduate Women," *Journal of Counseling Psychology* 35, no. 4 (1988).
5. Kim Chernin, *The Hungry Self: Women, Eating, and Identity* (New York: Harper & Row, 1985).
6. An interview with Diane Mickley, M.D., September 1989.
7. Gerald F. M. Russell, George I. Szmukler, Christopher Dare, and I. Eisler, "An Evaluation of Family Therapy in Anorexia Nervosa and Bulimia Nervosa," *Archives of General Psychiatry* 44 (1987).
8. Interview with Diane Mickley.

CHAPTER 8

1. Robert Cairns, Beverley D. Cairns, Holly J. Neckerman, Lynda L. Ferguson, and Jean-Louis Gariepy, "Growth and Aggression, Childhood to Early Adolescence," *Developmental Psychology* 25, no. 2 (1989).
2. James Youniss and Jacqueline Smollar, *Adolescent Relations with Mothers, Fathers, and Friends* (Chicago: University of Chicago Press, 1985).
3. Laurence Steinberg and Susan Silverberg, "The Vicissitudes of Autonomy in Early Adolescence," *Child Development* 57 (1986).

CHAPTER 9

1. Douglas C. Kimmel and Irving B. Weiner, *Adolescence: A Developmental Transition* (Hillside, N.J.: Lawrence Erlbaum, 1985).
2. Jack Block, Jeanne H. Block, and Susan Keyes, "Longitudinally Foretelling Drug Usage in Adolescence: Early Childhood Personality and Environmental Precursors," *Child Development* 59 (1988).
3. Laurie Chassin, Clark C. Presson, and Steven J. Sherman, " 'Constructive' vs. 'Destructive' Behavior in Adolescent Health-Related Behaviors," *Journal of Youth and Adolescence* 18 (1989).
4. Judith S. Brook, Martin Whiteman, and Ann S. Gordon, "Stages of Drug Use in Adolescence: Personality, Peer, and Family Correlates," *Developmental Psychology* 19 (1983).
5. Harold M. Voth, M.D., and Gabriel G. Nahas, M.D., *How to Save Your Child from Drugs* (Middlebury, Vt.: Paul Eriksson, 1987).
6. Ken Barun, *When Saying No Isn't Enough* (New York: Penguin Books, 1989).

CHAPTER 10

1. Kristen A. Moore, James L. Peterson, and Frank F. Furstenberg, "Parental Attitudes and the Occurrence of Early Sexual Activity," *Journal of Marriage and the Family* 48 (1986).
2. *Teen Pregnancy Prevention Programs: What Have We Learned?* (Washington, D.C.: Family Impact Seminar, American Association for Marriage and Family Therapy, Research and Education Foundation, May 1989).
3. Greer Litton Fox and Christine Medlin, "Accuracy in Mothers' Perception of Daughters' Level of Sexual Involvement: Black and White Single Mothers and Their Teenage Daughters," *Family Perspectives* 20, no. 4 (1987).
4. *What About the Boys? Teenage Pregnancy Prevention Strategies* (Washington, D.C.: Children's Defense Fund, Adolescent Pregnancy Prevention Clearing House, July 1988).

5. Melvin Zelnik and Farida K. Shah, "First Intercourse Among Young Americans," *Family Planning Perspectives* 15 (1983).

6. C. D. Hayes, *Risking the Future: Adolescent Sexuality, Pregnancy and Childbearing*, final report of the National Research Council's Panel on Adolescent Pregnancy and Childbearing, Vol. 1 (Washington, D.C.: National Academy Press, 1987).

7. Brent C. Miller, J. Kelly McCoy, Terrance D. Olson, and Christopher M. Wallace, "Parental Discipline and Control Attempts in Relation to Adolescent Sexual Attitudes and Behavior," *Journal of Marriage and the Family* 48 (1986).

8. Greer Litton Fox, *Intrafamilial Sexual Socialization: Patterns and Outcomes*, final report to U.S. Department of Health and Human Services, Office of Adolescent Pregnancy Programs, 1986.

CHAPTER 11

1. Ruthellen Josselson, "Ego Development in Adolescence," in J. Adelson, ed., *Handbook of Adolescent Psychology* (New York: John Wiley and Sons, 1980).

2. Jeanne Brooks-Gunn and Marta Zahaykevich, "Parent and Adolescent Daughter Relationships in Early Adolescence: A Developmental Perspective," in K. Kreppner and R. Lerner, eds., *Family Styles and Life-Span Development* (Hillsdale, N.J.: Lawrence Erlbaum, 1988).

3. John R. Buri, Lynda M. Richtsmeier, and Karen K. Komar, "Forgiveness as a Psychological Antecedent of Perceived Parental Nurturance," paper presented at the 97th Annual Convention of the American Psychological Association, New Orleans, 1989.

4. Diana Baumrind, "The Influence of Parenting Style on Adolescent Competence and Problem Behavior."

Index